A UNITED NATIONS
PARLIAMENTARY ASSEMBLY

'In this time of despair and confusion, this paper is a clear statement on the feasibility of a more sustainable, fair and democratic political structure to cope with the issues of a global world. The theoretical and practical aspects of a UN Parliamentary Assembly are analyzed and developed with precision and accuracy. It's a fundamental contribution to the politics of the 21st century.'

—**Fernando Iglesias**, Argentine Deputy and President, World Federalist Movement

'A UN Parliamentary Assembly is an important pragmatic step that needs to be taken now. This assembly should pave the way for a global constitutional process and eventually transition into a real world parliament.'

—**Daniel Jositsch**, Swiss Senator and Professor of Law

'The UN needs reforms and new mechanisms for more democratic and efficient decision-making. A Parliamentary Assembly would stimulate global solutions for global problems and better connect the UN with the citizens. This study shows how it can work.'

—**Jo Leinen**, Honorary President, European Movement International; former State Minister for the Environment and former Member of the European Parliament

'This study includes important recommendations and reflections on how a UN Parliamentary Assembly can be implemented and evolve over time. This new assembly is necessary to improve the democratic character of the United Nations and global governance.'

—**Livingstone Sewanyana**, UN Independent Expert on the promotion of a democratic and equitable international order

'This report illustrates that a UN Parliamentary Assembly can be crucial to achieve more inclusive global governance. I'm delighted to support this project.'

—**Achyuta Samanta**, Member of the Lok Sabha and founder, Kalinga Institute of Industrial Technology & Kalinga Institute of Social Sciences, India

'The vision of a world parliament is giving hope and direction. The UN needs a democratic body that can make global law to the benefit of all. This study is a key resource that explains how this can be put on track.'

—**Ivone Soares**, Member of Parliament, Mozambique

'A United Nations Parliamentary Assembly is essential reading for all of those who have been studying or working for global democracy. In providing a roadmap for the creation of the assembly, Brauer and Bummel remind us that setting the stage for a humane future is not only desirable but eminently feasible.'

—**Andrew Strauss**, Dean and Professor of Law, University of Dayton School of Law

ABOUT THIS PUBLICATION

The creation of a UN Parliamentary Assembly as an initial step towards a world parliament is a key goal of Democracy Without Borders. This study examines the proposal and presents official recommendations.

ABOUT THE PUBLISHER

DEMOCRACY WITHOUT BORDERS is an international civil society organization with chapters around the world that promotes democracy from the local to the global level with a focus on strengthening democratic participation and representation of citizens in more effective global institutions. Democracy Without Borders coordinates the international Campaign for a UN Parliamentary Assembly.

ABOUT THE AUTHORS

MAJA BRAUER is a board member of Democracy Without Borders in Germany. She has studied philosophy and political sciences and completed a PhD on the subject of world federalism.

ANDREAS BUMMEL is director of Democracy Without Borders and of the Campaign for a UN Parliamentary Assembly. He was trained in business administration and studied law.

A UNITED NATIONS PARLIAMENTARY ASSEMBLY

A policy review by
Democracy Without Borders

Maja Brauer
Andreas Bummel

We wish to thank The Workable World Trust
for their kind support.

Cover by Belinda Designs

Front: Possible logo of a UN Parliamentary Assembly
created by Tony Fleming, CC BY-SA 3.0

Back: Boutros-Ghali made this statement on
16 May 2007 in a message to the Campaign for a
UN Parliamentary Assembly

Paperback ISBN 978-3-942282-17-8
Hardcover ISBN 978-3-942282-18-5
Ebook ISBN 978-3-942282-19-2

Visit our website at
www.democracywithoutborders.org

Contents

Abbreviations

ASEAN	Association of Southeast Asian Nations
AU	African Union
COSAC	Conference of Parliamentary Committees for Union Affairs of Parliaments of the European Union
CUNPA	Campaign for a United Nations Parliamentary Assembly
DWB	Democracy Without Borders
EALA	East African Legislative Assembly
ECOSOC	United Nations Economic and Social Council
EP	European Parliament
EU	European Union
GPA	Global Parliamentary Assembly
GRULAC	Group of Latin American and Caribbean Countries
ICC	International Criminal Court
ICJ	International Court of Justice
ILO	International Labour Organization
IPI	International Parliamentary Institution
IPU	Inter-Parliamentary Union
IMF	International Monetary Fund
MEP	Member of the European Parliament
MP	Member of Parliament
NATO	North Atlantic Treaty Organization
NGO	Non-governmental organization
OSCE	Organization for Security and Co-operation in Europe
P5	The five permanent members of the UN Security Council
PACE	Parliamentary Assembly of the Council of Europe
PAP	Pan-African Parliament
SDG	Sustainable Development Goal
UDHR	Universal Declaration of Human Rights
UN	United Nations
UNFCCC	United Nations Framework Convention on Climate Change
UNPA	United Nations Parliamentary Assembly
UNPN	United Nations Parliamentary Network
UNWCI	United Nations World Citizens' Initiative
WTO	World Trade Organization

Preface

The 75th anniversary of the UN coincides with a dramatic global health crisis caused by the coronavirus pandemic and exacerbated by an incoherent, slow and insufficient global response. This is another symptom of an underlying crisis of global governance. The traditional intergovernmental approach to global challenges is failing. Global warming is an example: action over the last thirty years has been ineffective. Scientists tell us that not much time is left, if any, to prevent a runaway climate crisis.

The root cause of this ineffective governance is a scale mismatch between a political order based on nation-states and issues demanding decisive planetary action. What is needed is a new vision of a democratic world order that is based on shared global sovereignty for global issues. In the current context of nationalist populism, geopolitical tensions, and rising authoritarianism, the goal of a new UN, based on supranational global decision-making with real authority, will not be realized overnight. Nonetheless, whilst it is true that the world is faced with many acute problems requiring immediate action, it would be a big mistake not to pursue long-term systemic change in parallel. Transformation of today's dysfunctional global system is long overdue. We are convinced that setting up a UN Parliamentary Assembly represents the single most important step towards this.

The proposal of a UN Parliamentary Assembly as described in this study is pragmatic and achievable under current conditions. We envision a modest start that paves the way to incremental development, eventually leading to a transition of the assembly to a directly elected world parliament in connection with an overhaul of the UN and related institutions. The quicker this happens, the better. In the meantime, even in its initial stage, a UNPA has the potential to bring about powerful change.

This study presents official recommendations and conclusions endorsed by Democracy Without Borders as an organization. These are summarized at the beginning and explained later in the main body of the publication. This assessment draws on previous official documents[1] and the authors have at-

---

[1] In particular Bummel, 2010a and 2010b, as well as all CUNPA documents in the annex.

tempted to take into consideration arguments raised in consultations and discussions on the subject over the years. We thank all who participated in such debates and in the project of advocating a UNPA in one way or another over time. It is impossible to mention all by name. For their ongoing and longtime support in advocating a UNPA particular thanks are owed to Jo Leinen, Fernando Iglesias, Ivone Soares, Fergus Watt, and Nancy Dunlavy.

We wish to thank Jessica Seiler and her team who translated the initial draft of this document from German into English and those who checked sections of the language. Special thanks go to John Vlasto who checked the language of the entire document and in addition provided substantive feedback. We are grateful to all who took the time to read the draft and provide remarks and comments. Any flaws and errors remaining are our own.

This publication is dedicated to the memory of Joseph Schwartzberg who passed away at the age of 90 in 2018. Through the Workable World Trust that he created in 2014, Joe has made substantial contributions to support the work of Democracy Without Borders, for which we are immensely grateful. Joe was a strong advocate of a UN Parliamentary Assembly and made intellectual contributions of his own, too. In 2012, for instance, our predecessor organization published a study authored by him on the allocation of seats in a UNPA.[2] We wholeheartedly agree with the premise underlying his main work that the design of decision-making institutions has an important bearing on the quality and legitimacy of the decisions they make.[3]

Finally, we wish to invite readers to provide feedback and to engage in a discussion. Since it was first put forward in 1949, the concept of a UNPA has evolved and will continue to do so. If you agree with the main thrust of the proposal as presented here, please consider supporting Democracy Without Borders and join our efforts.

---

[2] Schwartzberg, 2012.
[3] Schwartzberg, 2013, p. 2.

Executive Summary

Humanity faces a multitude of global challenges, above all the need to create a sustainable, just and peaceful global civilization that respects planetary boundaries and preserves life on Earth.

The present existential global threats can only be tackled if global institutions and political processes are strengthened and renewed. They must derive their legitimacy from the people and empower them to work together for the global common good and future generations.

This requires implementing democratic representation and participation at the global level. To initiate this democratization and strengthening of global governance, this study calls for the creation of a UN Parliamentary Assembly and presents official recommendations of Democracy Without Borders.

The assembly can be designed along the lines of existing international parliamentary institutions and at the outset be established by the UN General Assembly as a complementary body without the need to amend the UN Charter.

The powers and functions of the assembly should be expanded gradually with the long-term objective of developing a world parliament whose members are elected directly by the global population.

Initially, representatives should be selected by political groups in existing parliaments whereby the opposition is to be represented.

It is recommended that the assembly is open to universal participation and that the allocation of seats per country should initially follow the principle of degressive proportionality. The work is to be based on transnational political groups formed by individual representatives.

The assembly, political groups and individual representatives need to be committed to the fundamental principles of the UN Charter and the Universal Declaration of Human Rights.

Overview of conclusions and recommendations

Political objectives

- To involve the people of the world in the work of the UN and the system of global governance as well as in political negotiations and decisions at the global level through elected representatives.

- To exercise parliamentary oversight functions over the work of the UN and the system of global governance and to make its activities more transparent and accountable to the public.

- To establish a common platform for international parliamentary collaboration in the common interest of humanity.

- To provide an independent world forum in which potential solutions to global challenges are publicly discussed and recommendations for action are made to the UN and to governments.

- To promote fundamental human rights, democracy, and the rule of law worldwide and to contribute to the ongoing development of a planetary ethos that places the welfare of people and life on Earth at the centre.

- To serve as a catalyst for global democratization, integration, and reform.

Guiding principles

- *Universality:* The UNPA is open to all UN member states which have a parliament that is enshrined in the constitution and independent of the executive.

- *Representation of the people:* The members of the UNPA are not delegates of governments bound by instructions, but representatives of the world population legitimized by indirect or direct elections.

- *Representativeness:* The assembly reflects the spectrum of political opinion in a given country as accurately as possible. In case of indirect elections, in addition to ruling parliamentary groups, opposition parties represented in parliament also send delegates. In case of direct elections, a system of proportional representation is implemented.

- *Global mandate:* Parliamentarians have a statutory duty to represent the interests of humanity as a whole, to promote planetary unity and welfare and they have the mandate to discuss global issues and make recommendations in this regard.

- *Public deliberations and work in committees:* Based on the example of existing parliaments, regular public sessions are held and substantive work is accomplished through a system of committees and other bodies.

- *Transnational groups:* The working methods and procedures of the assembly are primarily based on transnational political groups that are established by the delegates according to common perspectives. These groups need to include members of a minimum number of states from a minimum of world regions.

- *Institutionalized network:* The UNPA is a platform to support an ongoing exchange between parliaments, international institutions, and civil society.

- *Co-option:* In order to improve the participation of minorities, opposition parties, and civil society, the political groups within the UNPA can co-opt at the committee level a certain number of persons as consultative UNPA members without voting rights.

- *Evolutionary development:* Similar to existing IPIs, the new UN assembly will initially only be endowed with limited advisory, supervisory, and participatory powers. However, these can and should be substantially expanded over time.

Establishment

A UNPA can be created in different ways. In our view, the most promising approach at this time is to establish the assembly as a *new subsidiary organ of the General Assembly under Article 22 of the UN Charter*. This assessment is based on the following:

- The procedure has been applied several times to establish new UN organs.

- A majority vote of the General Assembly is sufficient.

- The affiliation to the General Assembly puts the UNPA at the centre of the UN system.

- The status as a UN subsidiary organ enables the performance of a comprehensive spectrum of global tasks as well as the independence indispensable for parliamentary work.

- The annual sessions of the General Assembly allow for a continuous assessment and further development of the assembly.

Other procedures for the establishment of a UNPA that should continue to be evaluated are the negotiation of an international treaty or the upgrading of a parliamentary network previously established at the UN as a preliminary step. With regard to the Inter-Parliamentary Union (IPU), we advocate a complementary relationship with a UNPA as both bodies fulfill different functions. To strengthen the participation of civil society in the UN, we propose that the establishment of a global UN forum of civil society as an additional body besides a UNPA should be examined.

In case of Charter reform, we promote a global two-chamber system in which states and the people are represented in separate assemblies entrusted with the responsibility and endowed with the power to tackle political issues that can best be addressed at the global level, based on the principle of subsidiarity.

The primary goal should be an inclusive and transparent consultation and negotiation process on the establishment of a UNPA under the auspices of the UN. We think that it is expedient to decide on the best procedure to create the UNPA under international law in the course of these negotiations.

A UNPA as a driving force of democracy

If a UNPA is supposed to be globally inclusive, states with limited standards regarding democracy and the rule of law will have to be represented in it as well, like in existing IPIs. Being aware that the participation of such states affects the democratic legitimacy and reputation of the assembly, we nevertheless recommend a *universal approach*.

In our opinion there are strong reasons to expect that a UNPA open to all UN member states will still function in a democratic manner and furthermore evolve into a driving force for worldwide democratization. Among other things, this assumption is based on the democratic, rights-based, independent, and transnational character of the UNPA which is to be guaranteed and reinforced by its statutes and regulations. We consider the following essential:

- An unequivocal commitment of the UNPA as well as its individual members and political groups to the fundamental objectives of the UN Charter and the Universal Declaration of Human Rights (UDHR) in the statutes.

- A central procedural role of transnational political groups.

- Stipulating the incompatibility of holding a seat in the UNPA with government offices and high-ranking positions in civil service, including intergovernmental organizations.

- A regulation stating that during their tenure, UNPA delegates cannot be removed from office by institutions of their country of origin and enjoy protection.

- The establishment of an independent commission of inquiry to investigate potential allegations of corruption or other criminal activities.

- A verifiable code of conduct with regard to other employment of delegates and their ties to lobbyists; and the establishment of a transparency register.

- The objective of a universal transition to direct elections.

Election procedure

In the initial stage of the development of a UNPA, delegates may be sent by the parliaments of member states and possibly regional parliaments. Implementation of direct elections should be possible at any time. We recommend that at first, each country may decide on its own when to implement direct elections. However, the objective of general direct elections in all states should be enshrined in the statutes from the outset.

Initially, UN member states should constitute the framework for the organization of elections, whereas the necessary degree of homogeneity and transparency is ensured by general electoral rules. We propose that proportional representation should be implemented in order to have a broad political spectrum reflected.

We consider the following elements as cornerstones of the electoral rules:

- Regulations for the election of UNPA delegates by parliaments and by popular vote, as well as for the transition between these procedures.

- A procedure for the representation of the parliamentary opposition of all countries in case of indirect elections.

- Determination of the election period. To reduce cost and lower the threshold for a gradual introduction of popular elections we suggest that direct elections initially are held in conjunction with relevant national elections at the discretion of member states and not at a uniform global date.

- Provisions to achieve gender equality, beginning with the step of establishing procedures based on a minimum quota.

- An independent electoral commission that oversees the orderly implementation of elections and can impose sanctions.

- The involvement of existing IPIs in the assembly, for instance through their representation by consultative UNPA delegates.

A graduated allocation of seats

In order to balance the share of delegates coming from large and small countries in the assembly, the allocation of seats should be scaled. We recommend the following guidelines:

- The application of the principle of degressive proportionality aligned with the population size of countries.

- No drawing on economic power as a criterion to determine the number of seats allocated to a country in a UNPA.

- The application of universal and transparent criteria.

- A minimum number of two seats for all states to enable the representation of the parliamentary opposition of each country.

- A maximum total of seats within the range of 700 to 900 to guarantee the assembly's efficiency.

Representation of the opposition

- In the case of an election by parliaments, the political parties or groups represented should autonomously decide on the selection of the UNPA delegates apportioned to them.

- The number of UNPA seats allocated to each party or group should reflect their proportionate strength in the respective parliament as accurately as possible.

- At least one seat should be allocated to the largest parliamentary opposition group.

- In the case of direct elections, the parties or groups of a country draw up their own lists of candidates.

Powers and functions

A UNPA can perform a broad spectrum of tasks. Once the assembly is established or in the course of its empowerment, it should be entrusted with the following powers and functions, among others:

- Regular public plenary and committee sessions.

- Providing advice to the UN General Assembly and other UN institutions and participating in their work.

- Parliamentary oversight and control over the UN system, including the rights to submit questions, to receive information, and to summon witnesses as well as the possibility of setting up committees of inquiry.

- Participation in the preparation of the UN budget and in the election of the Secretary-General and other high-level officials of the UN system.

- Monitoring of major global developments and the implementation of UN programmes.

- Participation in treaty negotiations and international conferences under the UN umbrella.

- Regular public reports on the work of the UN system, with the possibility of holding hearings on specific issues.

- Organization of international expert meetings and public events.

- Coordination functions vis-à-vis the UN, other international institutions, parliaments, IPIs and civil society.

- Development of programmes to strengthen rule of law as well as democratic and sustainable social structures in the world.

- One priority of the assembly should be to organize global debates on ways to reform and transform the UN and the current mechanisms of global governance and to present proposals in this regard.

Organization and working procedures

We recommend that the plenary sessions of the UNPA take place at least twice a year in the form of session periods of several weeks, one of them during the opening sessions of the annual UN General Assembly.

The advisory and coordinating role of the UNPA should be embedded in continuous substantive work on global issues, setting priorities through the establishment of committees.

We stress the need for comprehensive and efficient procedures to involve citizens, civil society, and local administrations such as cities and municipalities.

Possibilities to supplement parliamentary work with innovative forms of citizen participation, such as online procedures, should be examined.

Financing

The amount of financing a UNPA will need depends on its assigned functions and whether delegates are selected by parliaments or by direct election.

If delegates are selected by parliaments, we estimate a minimum budget of 20 to 35 million US-Dollar which can be provided from the general UN budget and/or through voluntary contributions.

With the introduction of direct elections, the financial requirements increase. To cover the resulting costs, we recommend that in addition to a core budget, from which the actual tasks of the UNPA are financed, a supplementary budget should be established, which is to be funded by those states opting for direct elections.

If voluntary contributions are made by governments, international organizations, individuals, companies and other legal entities, the independence of the assembly must be guaranteed.

Prospects for development

A key characteristic of the UNPA concept is the combination of a pragmatically limited reform approach with a comprehensive vision of global development. A UNPA can be realized relatively easily and at a reasonable cost through proven procedures for the creation of international bodies. Once established, it can not only fulfil a variety of important functions within the global system, but over time also contribute significantly to its further development in the interest of the global community.

Elected officials can play a leading role in the gradual evolution of the UNPA into a global parliament directly elected by the world population and empowered to tackle global challenges.

We see a UNPA as a first, but vital step that for the first time gives people and the human community a voice at the global level and paves the way for a reform process in which the people of the world can gradually empower themselves and build a sustainable, just and peaceful world.

1. A voice of humanity

1.1. The failure of global governance

Never in the history of humankind has global interconnectedness been greater than today.[4] States, economic and social organizations, and individual people are becoming ever more closely linked in complex interdependencies that span the entire globe. Globalization has enabled an enormous increase in economic performance and prosperity in many parts of the world. But the global civilization that has emerged across national borders is fragile and vulnerable.

Human activity propelled by industrialization, modernization, urbanization, population growth and technological advancement has a dramatic global impact on the climate system, the biosphere and life on Earth. Global warming caused by the emission of greenhouse gas will lead to a catastrophic breakdown of the life-sustaining and safe operating space of humanity that existed over the past 11,000 years of human civilization.[5]

From both a political and a regulatory point of view, humanity is not only unprepared for the climate crisis, but also with regard to rapid, interconnected technological developments in the fields of bio- and nanotechnology, robotics, automation, and artificial intelligence. Increasingly, developments in the global system affect the realization of fundamental societal objectives such as political freedom, security, prosperity, ecological stability and sustainability.

The comprehensive global interdependence as well as the complex and problematic developments associated with it have significantly increased the need for global coordination, regulation, and organization. States are confronted with a multitude of problems that transcend national boundaries and political tasks that they cannot successfully tackle on their own. Therefore, more and more decisions on major policy issues have to be coordinated and taken at the international level.

Cross-border cooperation still mainly happens within the framework of intergovernmental organizations and forums that overlap without forming a coherent global governance architecture. This conglomerate has proven to be

---

4   Altman et al., 2019.
5   Rockström et al., 2009.

insufficient to meet the level of cooperation necessary to address global challenges. At the same time, the paradigm of state sovereignty, which has been handed down from the age of absolutism to the 21st century, perpetuates highly dangerous deficiencies of the international system. Effective action for the benefit of all is obstructed by the plurality of national interests. Due to their competition, services that are necessary to maintain global stability and development and to provide global public goods are provided only hesitantly and insufficiently. No government can expect that an advantage it renounces in favour of the long-term global common good will not be seized by other states. In this situation, the national interest imposes itself as a guiding principle for foreign policy. Moreover, a paralysis emerges that works against the realization of the public interest and contributes to undermining multilateral efforts.

Virtually all states still maintain a military apparatus and are in geopolitical competition with each other. The objective of comprehensive conventional and nuclear disarmament seems unattainable under the reservation of unrestricted national sovereignty. A particularly bitter example for the deadlock of global governance is the issue of global climate change, which constitutes an existential crisis where every year matters in terms of the necessary countermeasures. Nevertheless, the issue did not make it onto the global political agenda until 1992 in Rio de Janeiro. Crucial time was wasted. A marathon of international negotiations lasting for decades ensued. Its outcome is still uncertain, considering the USA's withdrawal from the Paris Climate Agreement and new record highs in annual CO_2 emissions.

The deficits and dangers inherent in the systemic compulsion to steer globalized processes in a multipolar way are further aggravated by the emergence of new centres of power. Multinational corporations and financial service providers operating at a global level can not only evade state control to a large extent, but also exert considerable influence on policies. Some of the serious problems associated with this increasing impact of corporate actors are the enormous outflow of capital to tax havens, the concealment of ownership structures by shell companies, the circumvention of social and environmental standards, extreme inequality, the development of a parallel world of financial transactions beyond the economic creation of value, and a fragmented economic and financial governance, hardly capable of dealing with the danger of shocks to the global economic system like the 2008 financial crisis.

As the ongoing debate about winners and losers of globalization illustrates, this development is associated with considerable social tensions and divisions, while at the same time options for joint action continue to erode. The perception of being economically, socially, and culturally left behind by globalization is now manifesting itself in many countries in a turn towards nationalist and populist movements. This development threatens to disrupt the social order at a national and international level and to further weaken already fragile multilateral cooperation.

The growing governance deficits of the international system are also accompanied by an increasing democratic deficit. The multitude of multilateral structures and forums that serve international policy-making offer only marginal opportunities, if any, for democratic participation. They are usually opaque and largely dominated by government representatives. As a result, the relevance of a democratic public and the foundations of democratic institutions, such as parliaments within states, are being increasingly undermined as more and more tasks and decision-making processes are shifted from the national to the international level.[6]

This worldwide erosion of democracy can only be countered by extending the principles of democratic legitimacy and parliamentary representation to policy-making beyond the nation state. At the same time, this process will allow humanity to overcome fragmentation, achieve a new level of organization and address global challenges more effectively.

1.2. The proposal of a UN Parliamentary Assembly

As a first step towards implementing democratic representation and participation at the global level, we call for the establishment of a United Nations Parliamentary Assembly (UNPA). This new body would enable the involvement of the citizens of UN member states in political negotiations and decisions at the global level through elected representatives.

The concept follows a pragmatic and gradual approach based on experiences with a variety of existing international parliamentary institutions (IPIs), especially regional parliaments and parliamentary assemblies. Similar to other IPIs, the UNPA would at first be given advisory, supervisory and participatory powers which could be expanded over time. A wide range of responsibilities and tasks is conceivable without the need to interfere with national constitutional orders or legislation. The development of the European Parliament (EP) from a parliamentary body with limited powers to a supranational parliament constitutes an instructive analogy.

The proposal of a UNPA is as old as the UN itself, and calls for a world parliament have existed for much longer. Since the 1990s, a broader discussion has evolved at both the academic and the political level. We only briefly

---

[6]   Cf. Leinen & Bummel, 2018, p. 315ff.

touch upon the historical background and the debate here and refer to the book "A World Parliament: Governance and Democracy in the 21st Century" published in 2018 by Jo Leinen and Andreas Bummel for a detailed account.[7]

Shortly after the founding of the UN and inspired by the establishment of the Council of Europe and its Parliamentary Assembly (PACE), the US diplomat and international law expert Louis B. Sohn pointed out the possibility of using Article 22 of the Charter to create a UNPA.[8] In the decades of East-West confrontation, this proposal, like UN reforms in general, played hardly any role in political practice.[9] It only experienced a renaissance after the fall of the Berlin Wall and the wave of democratization that followed it. A paper presented by the World Federalist Movement in 1992, which developed the proposal in more detail, gave a decisive impetus.[10] The treatise written by Canadian Dieter Heinrich concluded that a consultative UNPA should be seen as the beginning of a development process towards a world parliament.[11]

The debate on a UNPA was underpinned by the growing number of international institutions that were equipped with parliamentary bodies, such as the OSCE in 1991.[12] Not least, the development of the EU and the EP was an important inspiration. High-level reform initiatives, experts, and civil society networks took up the concept of a consultative UNPA.[13] In 1996, UN Secretary-General Boutros Boutros-Ghali warned that "[d]emocracy within the State will diminish in importance if the process of democratization does not move forward at the international level".[14] After his term of office, he endorsed the objective of a UNPA, which he described as an "indispensable step to achieve democratic control of globalization".[15]

In order to unite support from politics and society for a UNPA, the international Campaign for a United Nations Parliamentary Assembly (CUNPA) was launched in 2007 under the auspices of Boutros-Ghali. Following the example of the Coalition for the International Criminal Court which played a major role in the creation of the International Criminal Court (ICC), it was established as an informal network that is neutral in terms of party politics and ideology, operating on the basis of agreed upon objectives. In an *Appeal*

---

[7]   Leinen & Bummel, 2018, ch. 2-9.
[8]   Ibid., p. 62ff. with further references.
[9]   But see for example the discussion in Sohn, 1970, p. 58-60 and p. 121ff.
[10] Heinrich, 2010.
[11] We will touch on this in more detail later. For a world parliament as part of a world republic: Höffe, 2002.
[12] See Kissling, 2011.
[13] Cf. for instance Childers & Urquhart, 1994, p. 176-181 with reference to Heinrich on p. 176. Commission on Global Governance, 1994, p. 285f., endorsed the approach as a medium-term objective.
[14] Boutros-Ghali, 1996, p. 19f.
[15] Boutros-Ghali, 2007.

for the establishment of a Parliamentary Assembly at the United Nations, the members of the campaign advocate for the "gradual implementation of democratic participation and representation on the global level", for which a UNPA is identified as a first "indispensable step" as well as a "political catalyst for further development of the international system and of international law".[16] The concept of a UNPA is considered a pragmatic and achievable approach with an extraordinary evolutionary potential.[17]

The campaign is coordinated by Democracy Without Borders (DWB).[18] Since its launch in 2007, support for a UNPA has grown significantly. More than 1,600 members of parliament from over 130 countries, hundreds of personalities from other areas of society as well as numerous civil society groups have signed the campaign's international appeal[19] and supported the establishment of a UNPA. Parliamentarians associated with the campaign continually take the initiative in national and regional parliaments to move the debate forward. An increased global coordination of these activities is being pursued. A statement published in 2018 warned that "the United Nations, the multilateral order and democracy" were under attack. In this context, a UNPA was demanded as part of a counter strategy to strengthen democracy.[20]

Statements and resolutions in favour of a UNPA have been adopted by the Millennium Forum of civil society (2000), the Latin American Parliament (2008), the Senate (2008) and the Chamber of Deputies of Argentina (2009), PACE (2009), the Parliament of Mercosur (2011), PAP (2007, 2016), the EP (2011, 2017, 2018), the East African Legislative Assembly (2013), and the virtual UN75 People's Forum (2020) among many others.[21]

1.3. "We the People" – The human right to democracy

A UNPA represents a global manifestation of the right to democracy. National and international democratization are interconnected processes that both depend on the engagement of civil society. Democratization of global social structures at all levels - indicating a new phase of global integration - is inconceivable without new efforts in all parts of the world and their transnational linking. As a legitimate common forum of humanity, a UNPA would

---

[16] CUNPA, 2007a.
[17] For an analysis of the potential socio-economic dynamic cf. Falk & Strauss, 2011.
[18] DWB emerged in 2017 from the Committee for a Democratic UN founded in 2003, among others.
[19] CUNPA, 2007a.
[20] CUNPA, 2018.
[21] Some of these documents are included in the annex.

have a prominent position to further strengthen and coordinate such endeavours. It could become the most important ally of all those who work for the right to democracy within and beyond the borders of the nation state.

On the basis of the Universal Declaration of Human Rights (UDHR) adopted by the UN General Assembly in 1948, democracy is considered an inalienable human right (Article 21) that must be protected through international structures. Article 28 of the declaration states that everyone "is entitled to a social and international order in which the rights and freedoms set forth in this declaration can be fully realized." There is a growing awareness that this right to democracy must not only be universally guaranteed and institutionally protected, but also includes the decision-making structures of the international system.[22]

In each of its sessions, the UN General Assembly now adopts a resolution for the "promotion of a democratic and equitable international order", reaffirming the right of all people to that order.[23] Furthermore, the resolution states that this requires "the promotion and consolidation of transparent, democratic, just and accountable international institutions in all areas of cooperation, in particular through the implementation of the principle of full and equal participation in their respective decision-making mechanisms." The Agenda 2030 adopted by the UN General Assembly demands "effective, accountable and inclusive institutions at all levels" in goal no. 16 as well as "responsive, inclusive, participatory and representative decision-making at all levels." Consequently, this must also include the global level.

Although decisions taken at the international level often have a major impact on people's daily lives, they only offer indirect opportunities for participation, which are furthermore difficult to access, limited, and ineffective. NGOs, opposition parties, and members of parliaments also continue to stand on the sidelines of decisions taken by government representatives. Even in contexts where intergovernmental processes are in principle open to input from civil society, "ordinary" citizens face enormous difficulties if they wish to voice their concerns at this level. In contrast, international lobby groups have the necessary resources and organization to assert their specific interests, thereby exerting an influence on national legislative processes.[24] The development of international agreements generally eludes the participation and control of parliaments. As a result of multilateral negotiations, international treaties can usually only be adopted or rejected in their entirety when ratified in

---

[22]   Cf. Leinen & Bummel, 2018, p. 312ff.
[23]   For the 73rd session see UN, 2018.
[24]   Cf. Spiegel, 2009, p. 235-240.

the respective parliament, without any involvement of its members in the negotiation process. Frequently, the opposition agrees to treaties put to a vote in order not to harm external relations. Exclusive intergovernmental negotiations thus anticipate the outcome of national ratification.[25]

This problem is exacerbated by the diversity of international decision-making bodies and formats. So-called club governance, which manifests itself in informal bodies such as the G20 or the G8, has gained great importance. "Governance by Clubs"[26] contributes to the fragmentation of international decision-making processes, rendering them unpredictable, non-transparent, and exclusive. The creation of a UNPA would be a decisive step in reducing the international democratic deficit and to realize the guarantee of the human right to democracy at a global level.

Representative surveys carried out in many parts of the world over the past decade indicate broad support for democracy across the globe. Democracy is now almost universally recognized as the only legitimate form of government. Even authoritarian regimes feel compelled to pay tribute to this appreciation by at least holding sham elections on a regular basis. At the same time, however, they prevent a genuine development of democracy.

The broad support for democracy among the global population, which is often around 80 percent or higher, also extends to countries under authoritarian government. However, there are differences in the assessment of what democracy means, including views that consider it to be compatible with authoritarian values and social structures.[27]

This strong support for the democratic form of government is accompanied by widespread dissatisfaction with its concrete implementation. The latter concerns both the opportunities to voice one's own concerns in politics, which are perceived as inadequate, and the overall outcomes of policy-making. This points to the urgency of supporting good governance through international measures and of addressing the social upheavals to which globalization has contributed. As representative surveys in many countries suggest, a majority of the world population is open to far more binding and effective global policies than those currently pursued and supported by national governments. Majorities in most countries support, for example, strong regulation of the arms trade, the complete abolition of nuclear weapons, an inter-

---

[25] Cf. Beyme, 1998, p. 21 ff., cf. also Leinen & Bummel, 2018, p. 315ff.
[26] Schneckener & Rinke, 2012.
[27] Wike et al., 2017. See also Norris, 2011.

national responsibility to protect in the event of serious human rights violations by governments, increased state expenditures to combat hunger and extreme poverty in the world, and decisive action against climate change.[28]

The establishment of a UNPA would support these expectations in two
ways. On the one hand, it would be a step towards democratically legitimizing
world politics and providing a better representation of the will of the people.
On the other hand, it would be able to serve as an acknowledged platform of
the global community to advance the realization of solutions guided by the
common good.

A representative survey conducted by the research institute GlobeScan on
behalf of the BBC actually demonstrated a clear majority in favour of the creation of a directly elected parliamentary assembly at the UN (see table 1). People were interviewed in 18 countries that cover 61 percent of the world's population. In one of the questions on the reform of the UN, the participants were
asked for their opinion on the "creation of a new UN Parliamentary Assembly, composed of directly elected representatives, with the same powers as the
UN General Assembly, which is controlled by national governments." On average, 63 percent supported the reform proposal, while 20 percent were
against it, and 17 percent were undecided.

A UNPA would represent people directly at the world level for the first
time, thus opening up the opportunity to get issues on the global political
agenda without the intermediary role of national governments. Moreover, it
would pave the way to make international bodies and decision-making processes more transparent and accountable.

Through the work of a global parliamentary assembly, it may also be ex-
emplified that democracy is not only a fundamental right that every single
person on earth is entitled to, but also a value that can only be realized collectively in connection with other fundamental human rights. The assembly
would thus lend significance to the first words of the UN Charter: "We the
peoples."

1.4. A parliamentary umbrella for international cooperation

A UNPA would be an institutional hinge between the UN and the system of
global governance, parliaments, governments, civil society, and citizens. In
this capacity, it could function as a political catalyst for the revitalization of
the UN and the further development of the international system as well as
international law.

---

[28] Kull, 2010. See also Global Challenges Foundation, 2017 and 2018.

Table 1: Results (in %) of a survey conducted on behalf of the BBC in 2005 in order of the share of positive responses per country: "Do you support the establishment of a new UN Parliamentary Assembly, comprising representatives elected directly by the people, with powers equivalent to those of the present UN General Assembly, which is controlled by national governments?"[29]

	Positive	Negative	Undecided
Mexico	80	5	15
Brazil	73	10	17
Indonesia	73	13	14
Italy	70	20	10
China	68	20	12
Argentina	66	29	6
Germany	66	24	9
Canada	65	28	8
Philippines	65	29	6
Chile	64	7	29
UK	64	28	8
South Korea	62	33	4
Poland	59	9	31
Australia	56	35	10
India	56	22	23
Turkey	55	18	28
USA	55	35	10
Russia	33	22	44

The UN provides an indispensable framework for strengthening international cooperation for the long-term global common good. With its numerous specialized agencies, the organization has been able to improve the lives of hundreds of millions of people. Furthermore, its role in the formulation of universal fundamental values and global political objectives is essential. The radiance of these norms results from their reference to the postulate of an inalienable equal dignity of all people, which received historical endorsement in the form of the UDHR.

However, as an intergovernmental organization based on the paradigms of state sovereignty and non-interference in internal affairs, the UN also reflects the systemic shortcomings of the international system, including the democratic deficit. Like other UN bodies, the General Assembly, as the plenary of all member states, consists of government representatives bound by directives who vote according to national interests. There is no direct democratic legitimation of these delegates through popular elections or parlia-

---

[29] GlobeScan Incorporated, 2005.

ments. Moreover, the resolutions adopted by the General Assembly only constitute recommendations, with which member states may or may not comply at their own discretion.

Since each state has one vote, microstates have the same weight in the assembly as populous great powers. Together with the non-binding nature of the resolutions, this is one of the reasons why key political decisions are often taken outside of the UN. In contrast, in the Security Council, which bears the "primary responsibility for the maintenance of international peace and security" (Article 24 of the Charter), an almost insurmountable structure of domination by five states has been installed. Based on Chapter VII, the Security Council can adopt legally binding resolutions. However, each of the five permanent members, the so-called P5, can block decisions by means of a veto right, which is exercised frequently. In addition, amendments to the UN Charter require their approval as well.

These fundamental democratic deficits cannot be essentially redressed by the efforts made within the UN so far. These measures include cooperation with the IPU as the international organization of parliaments and the accreditation of several thousand NGOs to the Economic and Social Council (ECOSOC). Moreover, opportunities for NGOs and individuals to participate in UN conferences (e.g. the Climate Change Conferences) and work processes (e.g. the Agenda 2030) are being provided. However, these options for participation are too selective, discontinuous, and peripheral to allow for a significant involvement of people in the UN decision-making processes. Parliamentary representation of the world population and direct accountability of UN bodies to the people are completely missing to date.

That the UN has not yet been supplemented by a representative organ of parliamentary participation and control is all the more remarkable as this very path has already been followed in many other intergovernmental institutions. Since the Second World War, many IPIs have emerged to counter the dissociation of parliaments and elected representatives from the political processes that have increasingly shifted to the international level. Since the 1990s, their number has risen rapidly. There are now over 100 and growing.[30]

IPIs enable the involvement of members of national parliaments in international activities, the exercise of supervisory functions over intergovernmental organizations and processes, and coordination between delegates from different countries. Many of these bodies have only a regional character, are issue-specific, and usually work far away from public perception. They

---

[30]   Cf. Kissling, 2011, p. 10; Cofelice, 2019; Rocabert et al., 2019; Schermers & Blokker, 2018, §§ 558-596.

have no legislative functions, with the exception of the EP and the East African Legislative Assembly (EALA).[31] Over time, many IPIs have acquired an extended spectrum of functions due to their increasing importance in international cooperation.[32] There are plans to transfer legislative powers to some IPIs, such as the Pan-African Parliament (PAP).

Together with the major economic and financial institutions - the WTO, World Bank, and IMF - the UN are, as the PAP criticized, one of the last international organizations "lacking an integrated and institutionalized Parliamentary Assembly."[33] The creation of a UNPA would complement the UN with parliamentary advice, control, participation, and coordination, as is already common in other intergovernmental institutions at the regional level.

Compared to other IPIs, a UNPA would have a preeminent position. Because of its global reach and its wide democratic legitimacy, it would be well-placed to be developed into the central umbrella for parliamentary cooperation at the global level. In this vein, a UNPA can constitute a global parliamentary body "that includes distinctive innovative features that go beyond the characteristics of existing national and regional assemblies and parliaments. Acting as an institutionalized 'network of networks', a UNPA could allow representatives of existing parliamentary networks and institutions to formally participate in its work, thus providing them with more leverage and influence."[34] Thus, a UNPA can help to improve the relationship between the UN and the numerous IPIs, create synergies between the activities of IPIs, and counter a fragmentation of the IPIs as well as of the international system.

The UNPA Secretariat could coordinate and coalesce parliamentary activities at all levels of the UN system. Moreover, the assembly would also be the ideal focal point for processing the results of parliamentary deliberations on specific topics, relaying them within the UN, and promoting the implementation of the respective recommendations over a long period of time. The UNPA would be the institutional memory of these activities.

1.5. A catalyst for integration and change

As an advisory, coordinating, and supervisory body, a UNPA does not immediately bring about a radical structural renewal of the international system, nor does it provide a guarantee for a more responsible global governance,

---

[31]   See Kissling, 2011, p. 41.
[32]   Ibid., p. 49f.
[33]   PAP, 2007.
[34]   CUNPA, 2013.

which remains largely in the hands of governments. Nevertheless, a UNPA can be expected to be highly politically relevant from the outset due to the integrative function it could develop within global society. A central world forum based on democratic legitimacy and fair representation would be an institution respected by people all over the world, where global problems are publicly discussed and tackled and where expert knowledge, creative solutions, and holistic views[35] are introduced to the global debate. Politicians would face increased public pressure for globally responsible action. At the same time, the representation of a broad spectrum of political views and the debates within the UNPA would open up improved prospects for an ongoing process of global education and opinion formation.

Through the discussions in the plenary and the work in the committees, the UNPA could develop into a global hub for the communication, exchange, and networking of innovative forces in politics and civil society. In this institutional context, politically active citizens from different countries, experts, and decision-makers from politics and society would be able to join forces in public debates and collaborative work as well as to present their concerns to global parliamentarians. At the same time, they could help advance political initiatives of the UNPA at different levels of society.

Promotion of a cosmopolitan and planetary ethos

A parliamentary assembly at the UN is much more than just another institution.[36] By its very existence and as a first step towards a world parliament, it would embody fundamental values and ideas as well as stipulate them as a benchmark for politics:

- Humanity is a democratic community that includes all people in their diversity.
- The notions of global citizenship and a direct relationship between all people and their planet.
- Democracy does not end at national borders and people have the right to decide on matters affecting them collectively at the global level.
- In addition to loyalty to one's country, there should be a cosmopolitan loyalty as a shared responsibility of each person to the planetary community.
- The world order is more than an arena of states and it requires a collective authority that represents the rights of all and their common good.

---

[35] For a holistic analysis of international and national law see Stamelos, 2020.
[36] Cf. Heinrich, 2010, p. 36.

A UNPA would not only be an expression, but also a catalyst of such a change in perception and awareness in international politics. Because of its transnational character, it would promote an earth- and citizen-centred perspective that incorporates a responsibility for future generations and life on our planet. As a forum of humanity, it can contribute to changing mindsets so that more and more people move beyond political and cultural boundaries, see themselves also as citizens of the world and unite for collaborative efforts to preserve their home planet earth.

Strengthening the relationship to the citizens

As an integral part of the UN, a UNPA would play an important role in complementing the work of the General Assembly and other organs of the UN system with parliamentary procedures. As the EP stated, a UNPA would help "increase the democratic character, the democratic accountability and the transparency of global governance and to allow for better citizen participation in the activities of the UN."[37] The elected representatives would be involved in international processes, could exercise advisory tasks, parliamentary control, and coordinating functions, and would regularly report on those activities to the global public and their voters. Through the members of the UNPA, the UN with its manifold functions would move closer to the population in the member states, gain better acceptance, and inspire renewed interest. The UNPA parliamentarians could take up concerns and ideas from citizens and introduce them into the activities of the UN, for instance through a committee on petitions.

Promotion of democracy

Democratically legitimized by a major part of the world population and centrally anchored in the global system, a UNPA embodies the claim that fundamental civil liberties and democratic representation are not only to be implemented everywhere on earth, but also beyond the borders of the nation state. This raises the expectation that the UNPA delegates will address approaches to strengthen democracy in the member states and at the international level. The expansion of existing IPIs, especially the parliamentary bodies of regional organizations, and the democratization of international structures should be on the agenda in this context. The same applies to opportunities to develop

---

[37] EP, 2018.

global democracy beyond representation and to involve people more directly in the work of the UN and other international organizations.[38]

Furthermore, a UNPA will increase the credibility of the UN in promoting national democratization. The very existence of parliamentary cooperation across national borders would increase the pressure to justify undemocratic practices in member states. The assembly can play an active role in this regard, for example by monitoring the democratic development in member states and by supporting transformation processes towards democratically organized societies; this also includes the possibility of election observation.

Strengthening of human rights

Notwithstanding the fact that a UNPA would be likely to include delegates from states with problematic human rights situations, the body can be expected to play an important role in the implementation of these rights. Human rights debates in the plenary and at the committee level can increase global public attention for those issues. Continuous monitoring of the human rights situation and substantive work to that end should be organized through a permanent human rights committee. Unlike government representatives to the UN Human Rights Council, the independent members of the assembly would have to show less consideration for government policy and the interstate relations of their home country. Therefore, they could address and criticize human rights violations more openly. In contrast, when NGO representatives accredited to the Human Rights Council or other UN bodies point out these violations, they must always fear that their organization's consultative status at the UN will be challenged.

The opportunities of the UNPA's work in support of human rights are further bolstered by the fact that delegates of opposition parties and advocates of minorities will be represented in a UNPA and can speak with their own voice. In this regard, the assembly can also create publicity by including representatives of indigenous or minority groups in its deliberations - without them necessarily having to be elected parliamentarians with voting rights - for example through co-option. Moreover, a standing committee on minority issues would also be possible. In addition, the assembly should be empowered to submit cases of serious human rights violations to the Security Council and to set up committees of inquiry.

As a complementary body to the UN General Assembly, a UNPA can also help strengthen this institution in the exercise of its subsidiary responsibility

---

[38]   A complementary approach is the instrument of a UN World Citizens' Initiative, see p. 104.

for the maintenance of international peace and security. If the Security Council fails to take action due to the threat or use of a veto by one or more permanent members, the General Assembly has reserved the right to do so itself.[39] If such a decision was not only supported by the General Assembly, but also by a UNPA, it would have strong political legitimacy. On this basis, the principle of the responsibility to protect could be strengthened despite the veto powers in the Security Council.

Supporting security, justice, sustainability, and good governance

Guaranteeing human rights and democracy is not possible without ensuring that people around the world can achieve their life goals in a safe, socially and environmentally sustainable surrounding. The history of the UN illustrates this realization. In 1948, the UDHR established the principle that political rights such as freedom of speech and freedom of conscience cannot be established and protected without sufficient attention to economic and social development. In 1972, the Stockholm Declaration established the principle that efforts to advance economic and social development around the world must be ecologically sustainable.

With a central position close to the decision-making centres of the UN and a broadly based representative character, a UNPA seems particularly suited to analyze pressing global challenges and to promote a worldwide discussion. It is also a suitable context to focus on holistic approaches in the interest of humanity that take the complex interrelationships between global problems into consideration. According to the ILO World Commission on the Social Dimension of Globalization, a Global Parliamentary Group should be "concerned with the coherence and consistency between global economic, social and environmental policies." [40] A UNPA could take over this function.

The debate and cooperation in a UNPA would be qualitatively different from the capacities hitherto provided by intergovernmental bodies and conferences. The reason for this difference is that delegates represented in this forum would be free to address difficult issues and develop global solutions without particular consideration of national interests and bilateral intergovernmental relations.[41]

Starting points for a substantive contribution of a UNPA to cope with the complex problems and challenges of our time have been set out by the UN in

---

[39] UN, 1950 ("Uniting for Peace").
[40] ILO, 2004, p. xiv.
[41] An example are violations of international law and human rights in drone warfare, cf. Leinen & Bummel, 2018, p. 216f.

its Agenda 2030. Accordingly, the EP called for the establishment of a UNPA "in particular, to contribute to the successful implementation of the UN Agenda 2030 and the SDGs."[42] A UNPA could monitor the development, implementation, and coordination of UN programmes and communicate their work to national parliaments and citizens. Under the leadership of a standing committee on sustainable development and the Agenda 2030, a UNPA could be integrated into the High-Level Political Forum (HLPF), which serves UN member states to review progress.

It would also be possible to set up committees to tackle international security issues, in particular the causes of and fight against international terrorism as well as disarmament.

Reform of the UN and the international system

Once established, a UNPA could "advocate and facilitate a reform of the present system of international institutions and global governance."[43] This would entail a focus on the existential question of how to shape a future system that is capable of reliably ensuring the well-being of all members of the human community for generations to come. How can the currently ineffective institutions of the international system be further developed to enable the inhabitants of planet earth and their political representatives to regulate their relations in a way that facilitates the establishment of a democratic, peaceful, just, and ecologically sustainable world order?

There are numerous proposals and initiatives for UN reform and competing interests that need to be negotiated. As the political representation of humanity as a whole, a UNPA represents a self-evident forum for such deliberations. It will be predestined and legitimized like no other body for the task of scrutinizing the structures of the world system, putting options for its development on the international agenda, and advancing change. A UNPA can contribute to identifying common systemic and structural causes of global problems as well as to working on their elimination.

By continuously promoting a broad debate at all levels of world society, a UNPA could become an engine of global democratization, integration, and change. UN parliamentarians would be in the position to combine the knowledge, creativity, and commitment of people from all over the world to create effective and democratic global governance.

---

[42]   EP, 2018.
[43]   CUNPA, 2010, point 6.

2. Pathways to a UNPA

The establishment of a global parliamentary assembly could come about in various ways. In our assessment, there are two main options at this time: the establishment as a subsidiary body of the General Assembly under Article 22 of the UN Charter or on the basis of a new intergovernmental treaty. In the long term, the assembly thus established could later be transformed into a directly elected legislative world parliament as a result of a conference to review the UN Charter in accordance with Article 109 of the UN Charter.[44]

Other approaches to the creation of a UNPA that have been discussed include the transformation of the Inter-Parliamentary Union (IPU), a body organized by civil society, as well as the establishment of a UN Parliamentary Network (UNPN) or a system of global parliamentary specialized committees as preliminary steps. In the following, we discuss these various proposals.

2.1. Amendment of the UN Charter

The most far-reaching option for establishing a world parliament at the UN is to amend the UN Charter according to the requirements set out in Articles 108 and 109. Within the framework of a successful Charter amendment, the parliamentary body could be established as a new main organ of the UN with far-reaching tasks and powers. Of primary importance would be enabling it to take decisions that are binding under international law in interaction with other organs like the General Assembly as the representation of member states. This option necessarily affects the institutional structure of the UN and the relationship between its bodies, and thus raises many fundamental questions. Moreover, the political and international legal hurdles that must be overcome in order to amend the Charter are very high.

On the basis of Article 109(1) of the Charter, a general conference to review the Charter may be convened by a two-thirds vote of the General Assembly and by decision of any nine members of the Security Council. According to Article 109(2), any amendment to the Charter recommended by the conference by a two-thirds majority shall enter into force as soon as it has

---

[44] Ibid., point 8.

been ratified by two-thirds of the members of the UN, including all of the P5. Any amendment to the Charter is thus subject to a veto right of the permanent members of the Council.

Article 109(3) provides that if a review conference was not placed on the agenda until the tenth annual session of the General Assembly following the entry into force of the Charter, i.e. in 1955, a simple majority vote of the General Assembly and of any seven members of the Security Council would be sufficient to do so. During the tenth General Assembly in 1955, this question was dealt with and a committee was set up to determine the time, place, and other modalities of a review conference. However, this never happened. From a legal perspective, a review conference could be convened according to the provisions of Article 109(3) at any time.

Article 109(3) of the UN Charter reflects the historic view that the international community has been granted the right to develop the structure of the world organization dominated by the victorious powers of the Second World War and to adapt the Charter to changing conditions. This holds more true today than ever before. Efforts to develop the UN into a world organization capable of meeting the demands of our time can point to and insist on the unfulfilled "San Francisco Promise".[45]

The hurdles for such a transformation of the UN are high. However, it is not unrealistic that convening a Charter Review Conference under Article 109(3) would initiate a comprehensive reform debate. Such a debate could in turn mobilize sufficient political pressure worldwide to ensure that the establishment of a UNPA within the course of Charter amendments would not only be approved by two-thirds of the UN member states, but ultimately also by the P5. As soon as it is possible to convene a general review conference or a series of such conferences in accordance with Article 109, the opportunity will open up to establish significant governmental functions at the global level in accordance with international law within a manageable time frame. These new functions would need to be linked to democratic participation and representation of the world population.

With a view to global decision-making procedures and the transition to a democratically legitimate world legislature, in the event of a fundamental reform of the UN Charter, we advocate the realization of a two-chamber system in which both the states and the citizens of the world are represented in separate assemblies.[46]

---

[45]   See Sharei, 2018 as well as the efforts of the Center for UN Constitutional Research, CUNCR.
[46]   So did Vaclav Havel, 2000, at the Millennium Summit. See also next ch. 2.2. and pp. 90f., 95 and 113.

Under the present circumstances, however, it is not foreseeable when and to what extent the political will necessary for a restructuring of the UN can be mobilized. A review conference should take place in a positive global political environment. Before such a conference is convened, a broad majority of governments should support strengthening and democratizing the world organization and the system of global governance on the basis of a commitment to human rights. Only then can it be ensured that the reform process that has been set in motion will produce satisfactory results and not actually lead to a weakening of multilateralism and the UN. Until then, measures below the threshold of a Charter amendment should be sought that promise chances of implementation even under difficult political conditions. A global parliamentary body set up as a precursor in this sense could help build the political foundations for a promising review conference.

2.2. A direct election of the General Assembly?

Under the UN Charter, the General Assembly is the UN's main body that brings together representatives of all UN member states. Primarily in the period following the UN's establishment it was suggested that instead of those delegates being appointed by governments, they could be directly elected by the citizens.[47] After being dormant for several decades, this idea has been taken up again recently.[48] At least partially it could be implemented without a Charter amendment as the Charter does not include any provisions on how delegates are to be selected. If they wanted to, individual states could decide to hold popular elections of their UN delegates. Such elections would have the potential to enhance the involvement of citizens in the work of the UN.

However, on the basis of the current UN Charter, even citizen-elected UN delegates would not be real representatives of the people, as they would still need to represent governments of UN member states and thus be bound by their instructions. A change of their mandate would require a major reconceptualization of the UN and the system of global governance. Moreover, the idea of an entirely citizen-elected UN General Assembly implies the long-term goal of democratizing all its member countries, too.

If understood as an *alternative path* to a UNPA, this proposal points in the direction of a global single-chamber system. This raises the question whether such a body is supposed to represent the interests of individual states or the global population as a whole. Representing both simultaneously is impossible.

---

[47] For example by Einstein, 1960 as well as Clark & Sohn, 1966, cf. p. xxi.
[48] Lopez-Claros et al. , 2020, ch. 4.

On the other hand, a global two-chamber system that includes an actual parliamentary body would allow for the representation of both states and citizens, drawing on important experiences with existing federal systems. Not least, the two chambers should have the ability to check and balance each other. Therefore, we consider two chambers as indispensable.[49]

However, the proposal could also be pursued *in addition* to setting up a UNPA and a two-chamber system. Existing federal political systems have different models to appoint representatives of constituent states' interests. Whereas members of the state governments take on this role in Germany, representatives are designated by the provincial parliaments in India and South Africa, and directly elected in Switzerland or the USA.[50]

While the General Assembly may be one of the most important main bodies of the UN's core organizations, it must still be taken into consideration that its current influence is limited and that it is only one of many intergovernmental conferences and bodies within and beyond the UN system that are constituted by different delegates which cannot all be directly elected. With that in mind, the issue of potential direct elections should be put in a long-term perspective, namely the context of a comprehensive reform that aims at streamlining, integrating, and improving the institutional coherence of existing structures.

Finally, the expected political benefit seems to be rather modest in comparison to the effort required. As the delegates in the General Assembly would continue to represent the interests of member states, their direct election would not be a significant step towards improving the representation of citizens compared to setting up an actual parliamentary body. In our view, efforts to democratize international relations based on this approach will only play a marginal role for the time being. Establishing a parliamentary body of the world population for the first time in history in the form of a UNPA would constitute a much better foundation for the democratization of international decision-making processes and structures.

2.3. Transformation of the Inter-Parliamentary Union?

One possibility under discussion for the creation of a UNPA is a transformation of the Inter-Parliamentary Union (IPU), which has been in existence

---

[49] In this regard, we follow Habermas, 1995, p. 308; Havel, 2000; and Höffe, 2002; cf. Leinen & Bummel, 2018, p. 381. See also pp. 90f., 95 and 113.

[50] For the first 125 years, the members of the US Senate were elected by state parliaments. Direct elections were introduced by the 17th constitutional amendment in 1911.

since 1889.[51] According to Article 1 of its statutes, the IPU views itself as "the international organization of the Parliaments of sovereign States". It currently has 179 full members, 12 associated international parliamentary organizations and some 70 organizations have observer status. It is noteworthy that the US withdrew at the end of the 1990s.

According to its statutes, the IPU is primarily pursuing the following objectives: to enhance the exchange of experience and the coordination between parliaments and parliamentarians, to deliberate on issues of international concern in order to initiate parliamentary activities in this regard, to promote the protection of human rights, and to further develop parliamentary institutions.

Parliaments themselves decide on the selection process to staff their delegations sent to the IPU's biannual assemblies. A specific term of office is not a requirement. Therefore, delegates can be appointed in an ad hoc manner, and the representatives of a country attending the assembly meetings often vary. Since the 1990s, an increasingly close cooperation between the IPU and the UN has developed, which is reflected in various cooperation agreements with the world organization and many of its specialized agencies.[52] At the Millennium Summit in 2000, the IPU was declared the organization predestined to occupy the parliamentary dimension of the UN.[53] In 2002, it was granted permanent observer status at the UN General Assembly and since then has been able to circulate its official documents in this context as well as to organize meetings and events at the UN. With a new cooperation agreement in 2016, the IPU has been granted further opportunities to participate in the work of the UN main committees, the subsidiary bodies of the General Assembly, and in UN conferences. However, such opportunities are to be determined on a case-by-case basis.

The IPU's specific organizational structure, its broad membership base, and its established cooperation with the UN seem to be a strong basis for a further development towards a UNPA, as has been suggested repeatedly.[54] Such a step could be taken in conjunction with a corresponding amendment of the IPU statutes by a decision of the General Assembly according to Article

---

[51] On this issue and a complementary relationship between the IPU and a UNPA cf. Bummel, 2019. About the role of the IPU in the debate on international reform and a UNPA that has been ongoing since the 1990s cf. Leinen & Bummel, 2018, ch. 7-9. Cf. also the discussion in Winter, 2005; Kissling, 2006 as well as Cabrera, 2018.

[52] Cf. Bummel, 2019, p. 5f. for what follows.

[53] Cf. UN, 2000, para. 30, item 10.

[54] Socialist International, 2003, section IV, no. 1; in 2005, the Liberal International considered the transformation of the IPU into a UNPA as a potential approach besides the procedure under Art. 22 UN Charter: Liberal International, 2005; cf. Bummel, 2019, p. 12f.; see also Deutscher Bundestag, 2005.

22 of the UN Charter. As a consequence, the IPU would become a subsidiary body of the General Assembly.

Another option would be an even closer connection to the UN by means of a renewed cooperation agreement granting the IPU more specific and expanded rights with regard to its function as a UNPA. This approach would preserve the IPU's organizational and financial autonomy, but just like the previously mentioned alternative, it would require a review of the IPU statutes as well as an overhaul of the organization's identity.

The process of selecting delegates would need to be fundamentally altered. They would have to be appointed individually by the parliaments or groups represented therein according to a general procedure and for a fixed term of office. Instead of the approximately equally sized national IPU delegations[55] and a scaled voting system,[56] a graduated system of seat distribution would balance the weight between large and small states. Moreover, representation would in principle no longer be based on a national and geopolitical grouping of delegates, but on their transnational organization according to common ideological and political views.

To date, a majority of the IPU membership has rejected the idea of developing the organization towards a global parliamentary body, a possibility that we initially endorsed. Moreover, the IPU's historical role in the efforts for a world parliament is ambivalent.[57] The then President of the German Bundestag, Norbert Lammert, declared at the IPU's Third World Conference of Speakers of Parliament in 2010 that the IPU is "neither a world parliament nor a subsidiary organization of the UN" and that it should also not become one.[58] This view became predominant. Furthermore, the IPU has opposed the EP's call for a Parliamentary Assembly at the WTO as well as the recommendation of the 2004 high-level Cardoso Panel to establish global parliamentary committees under the auspices of the UN.[59]

While the IPU has stood in the way of any complementary efforts so far, it has only developed the parliamentary dimension it claims – more or less exclusively – at the UN within a narrowly limited scope based on its mandate

---

[55] According to Art. 10(2) of the IPU Statute, there is only one differentiation regarding representation at the IPU Assembly: eight delegates for parliaments from states with less than 100 million inhabitants and ten for those from countries with more than 100 million inhabitants.

[56] Votes are allocated to member parliaments, not individual delegates, but delegations may split the allotted votes. The sliding scale of votes is stipulated in Art. 15(2) of the IPU Statute. Each parliament receives a minimum of ten votes, which are increased by up to 13 additional votes depending on the number of a state's inhabitants.

[57] Bummel, 2019, p. 12-14; cf. also Leinen & Bummel, 2018, p. 97-114, 328f.

[58] Quoted in ibid., p. 120.

[59] Ibid., p. 97f. and p. 108-110.

and structure as an umbrella organization of national parliaments. According to its own self-image, the parliamentary dimension of the UN should not primarily be implemented at the global level, but at the level of national parliaments.[60] The IPU's main concern is to strengthen national parliaments in dealing with international issues, not to fulfil parliamentary functions at a global level itself. It is therefore not surprising that the IPU neither exercises any supervisory functions over UN institutions nor has it sought to do so, regardless of all the cooperation agreements.

The IPU's rudimentary presence as a global actor is also due to the way its delegates are represented: namely primarily as delegates of national parliaments selected on an *ad hoc* basis and not mandated with a regular term of office for certain common functions. On the one hand, the organization's ties to the population are thus weak and consequently, the IPU can hardly be perceived as the people's representation at the UN. On these grounds, public attention for its work can be expected to remain low in the future. On the other hand, this also undermines the prospect of structurally linking the IPU to the current systems of global governance. The establishment of a permanent working relationship with other global institutions seems difficult to achieve given the constant redirection of parliamentary work on international issues to the level of individual national parliaments.[61]

Complementary relationship to a UNPA

The fundamentally different role of the IPU compared to a UNPA has been a subject of discussion. According to CUNPA, the IPU provides for a "parliamentary dimension to international cooperation" and strengthens national parliaments in the exercise of their supervisory function over national governments in international affairs. Conversely, it is characteristic of a UNPA that it would "exercise parliamentary functions directly at the international level in its own right". A UNPA would thus be at the same level as other international bodies and the UN bureaucracy. Whereas the role of the IPU would be as a "facilitator for the work of national parliaments", a UNPA would consist of "individual parliamentarians who would be called upon to take a global view".[62]

---

[60] Bummel, 2019, p. 7.
[61] In a comparative study of over 22 IPIs, Andrea Cofelice assesses the IPU as "a stand-alone institution, currently disconnected from any multi-actor complex governance system – a factor that irremediably hinders its capacity to develop the set of core functions dealing with international policymaking and accountability". Cofelice, 2019, p. 184.
[62] CUNPA, 2008.

A look at existing bodies at a regional level shows that the two institutions do not need to be mutually exclusive, but can rather complement each other in a constructive manner.[63] In Africa, for instance, there is the African Parliamentary Union - an organization similar to the IPU - as well as the Pan-African Parliament within the framework of the African Union as an international organization. While the former serves as a forum for national parliaments and consists of their representatives, the latter functions as a consultative parliamentary body of the African Union and is seeking supranational legislative powers. Corresponding equivalents can also be found in the EU: On the one hand, the EP exists as a directly elected representation of the EU population since 1979. On the other hand, the committees on European affairs of national parliaments are represented in the Conférence des Organes Specialisées sur les Affaire Communautaires (COSAC).[64]

Similarly, according to their specific orientation, a UNPA and the IPU would be able to fulfil complementary functions in relation to the UN and other institutions of global governance. Whereas the former would enable parliamentary oversight and democratic participation directly at the international level, the latter could continue to ensure the involvement of national parliaments in international affairs. This concept of a complementary relationship between IPU and UNPA is shared by various institutions. In 2011, the EP expressed the view "that a UNPA would be complementary to existing bodies, including the Inter-Parliamentary Union".[65] According to the PAP, the creation of a UNPA does not contradict the existing work of the IPU.[66]

A UNPA should be given dedicated parliamentary functions and rights in relation to the institutions of global governance. It is a proto-world parliament that should at least partially emerge from direct elections and represent humanity as a whole in a long-term perspective. However, the involvement of national parliaments will remain important in a future system. A UNPA should therefore be added as a supplementary institution while the IPU is maintained as the umbrella organization of national parliaments.[67]

---

[63]   Cf. Bummel, 2019, p. 10f.

[64]   COSAC was established in May 1989 in response to the weakening of the direct link between the EU and the members of parliament of the member states following the introduction of direct European elections. Before that, MEPs had been appointed by the national parliaments and could thus link the two levels themselves. Through COSAC, the role of the parliaments regarding the EU's common tasks was strengthened again.

[65]   EP, 2011; similar PACE, 2006 and Commission on Global Security, Justice & Governance, 2015, p. 86.

[66]   PAP, 2007, point 16.

[67]   Also recommended in Bummel, 2019.

Conclusion

Due to these considerations, we do not consider a transformation of the IPU into a UNPA an appropriate approach. A UNPA should be established in a different way and exist alongside the IPU. Both institutions should jointly operate as transnational nodes of parliamentary work. With this objective in mind, we consider it desirable to strengthen cooperation between all those forces, including the IPU and its members, that are committed to improving parliamentary influence on global transnational political processes.[68]

2.4. Transnational self-organization of civil society

Some advocates of global democracy have more faith in civil society taking matters into its own hands than in changing the existing structures of the world system, whether through a reform of the UN Charter or through international agreements. The idea is that communities across the globe connect with each other and demand rights of participation at the global level, thereby increasing public pressure for responsible global politics.

According to this approach,[69] high-ranking personalities from around the world could launch an appeal to set this process in motion. Once a critical mass of NGOs responds positively to such an initiative, international assemblies would be convened to establish a permanent forum of civil society or a kind of provisional self-appointed world parliament of delegates chosen through self-organized unofficial elections. Over time, this transnational assembly could gain in representativeness, geographical reach and political weight.

This approach is appealing because it avoids the big political hurdles that must be taken in order to achieve reforms of the current world system: The global structure is firmly based on nation-states and defended by existing national bureaucracies. Furthermore, it is supported by powerful interest groups, such as multinational corporations, which are often close to national governments and able to influence them for their own purposes.

Conversely, however, the independence of such a self-appointed body from established power structures of the world system represents an element that requires more reflection, and thus far this approach has received relatively little support. This independence entails a lack of political, legal, and

---

[68] PACE, 2006 underlines the role the IPU can play in cooperation with the UN in the establishment of a UNPA. On that note, it was also stated at the CUNPA meeting in Brussels in 2008 that "[t]he Campaign supports the work of the IPU and appreciates any and all active contributions from the IPU and IPU members in the efforts for the establishment of a UNPA." (CUNPA, 2008).

[69] Cf. Monbiot, 2004 as well as Falk & Strauss, 2011.

institutional connections to decision-making at the national and international levels, which leads to the question what specific influence the decisions and discussions of a symbolic world parliament of civil society would have beyond applying moral and political pressure. Such a forum may be a pioneer and incubator for a genuine and effective world parliament that actually takes part in decisions but it cannot replace it entirely.

The example of the World Social Forum raises the question whether global civil society is, both conceptually and in terms of necessary resources, capable of organizing a symbolic world parliament on its own for a sustained period of time. The World Social Forum, being a counter-weight to the World Economic Forum's annual meeting in Davos, initially received a great deal of attention and, as an open forum, was able to bring together forces of civil society. Now, however, it seems to have lost all influence.[70]

A world civil society forum

Parliamentary representation on the basis of universal suffrage on the one hand and civil society involvement on the other are interrelated but distinct ways of enabling the formation of public opinion and translating it into social action. It is their interaction that strengthens and keeps alive the democratic character of political decision-making processes. These two dimensions should not be mixed up, but rather anchored separately and linked to each other to achieve their common goals.

In order to increase civil society participation in the UN, we recommend that the establishment of a global civil society forum at the UN should be considered in addition to a UNPA. This aim could be pursued by the Conference of NGOs accredited to ECOSOC[71] and the NGO Major Group,[72] for instance. The NGO forum should be structured in such a way that it is able to represent the essential interests and perspectives of civil society actors in the most inclusive and fair way possible.

Convening a formal NGO assembly under UN auspices has been proposed several times. In 1994, for instance, the Commission on Global Governance advocated a civil society forum, consisting of NGOs accredited to the UN, that should meet annually in the run-up to the session of the UN General

---

[70]   Cf. Savio, 2019 and the contributions on greattransition.org/gti-forum/farewell-to-the-wsf.
[71]   Conference of Non-Governmental Organizations in Consultative Relationship with the United Nations, CoNGO (ngocongo.org).
[72]   The NGO Major Group is an association of civil society organizations that monitors the implementation of the Agenda 2030 (ngomg.org).

Assembly.[73] Another possibility is the above-mentioned approach of a forum organized by world society itself, which could be incorporated into the UN as soon as sufficient acceptance and representativeness have been achieved.

Other complementary initiatives

DWB supports initiatives aimed at improving the organization of civic interest in global democracy and reflecting this to political decision-makers. One way to express concern for global democracy are public activities that may gain impact through worldwide coordination.[74] Another example are simulated sessions of a UNPA or a world parliament that have already been carried out in several countries,[75] based on the successful and popular concept of "Model UN" simulations. Moreover, UN negotiations on a UNPA statute have been simulated.[76] Art projects can contribute to public attention as well.[77]

Finally, members of national parliaments and IPIs play an important role in providing new impetus to both politics and society. Their engagement with global democracy can link civil society to governments and international institutions. They can help shape not only policy, but also the national and global governance structures that support and channel it.[78]

A global online platform

A global online platform that is broadly used and accepted could prove to be a valuable tool to synergize efforts and enhance their political effectiveness. Moreover, the political work accomplished on this basis in itself could be a step towards global citizen participation and global democratization.

Such an internet platform should offer the best possible conditions for people and NGOs from different countries to network, coordinate on international issues, elect representatives, formulate common demands to politics

---

[73] Commission on Global Governance, 1995, p. 258-260.
[74] For instance the annual Global Week of Action for a World Parliament. During this initiative taking place on October 24 on the occasion of UN Day, public events and actions are organized in numerous countries under the auspices of DWB and other organizations. See DWB, 2019; (www.worldparliamentnow.org).
[75] Such as the Model Global Parliament in Australia that has been organized regularly since 2012, the 2019 Model UNPA in Argentina or the World Parliament Experiment taking place in Norway in 2007 and in Germany in 2008.
[76] Carried out in Halle, Germany in 2016.
[77] For instance the General Assembly organized by Milo Rau in Berlin in 2017 (www.general-assembly.net).
[78] For examples cf. Šabič, 2008, S. 264-66; see also Kissling, 2011. Associations like Parliamentarians for Global Action (PGA) or Parliamentarians for Nuclear Non-Proliferation and Disarmament (PNND) represent successful transnational initiatives of this kind.

and promote their public discussion. This requires generally-accepted, secure, and transparent procedures based on secure personal identification.[79]

In our view, such a virtual platform could make an important contribution to global mobilization, but it cannot replace the goal of a UNPA established and recognized by governments. An online platform that enjoys widespread support and sufficient public attention would be able to provide assistance in preparing and promoting the realization of a UNPA. The people and organizations collaborating in this context could make a significant contribution to raising public awareness for the necessity of democratization and parliamentarization of world politics as well as to increasing political pressure in support of its implementation.

2.5. Affiliation as an organ of a specialized organization

In principle, a UNPA can be set up as a specialized body to various institutions within and outside the UN system, but a closer look must be taken at the development opportunities that can be expected in each case.

Some of the most important institutions at the international level do not yet have a parliamentary body and proposals have been made to amend this, as for example for the WTO[80] and the UN Framework Convention on Climate Change (UNFCCC).[81]

This raises the question whether such a specialized parliamentary assembly might serve as the nucleus of a future UNPA with a global reach. Especially if it was attached to an institution whose decisions can have a major impact on the daily lives of the world's population, such as WTO, IMF, World Bank, or UNFCCC, it is conceivable that sufficient attention of the world public could be raised to put the assembly's development on the agenda.

If the project is successful, however, it will probably not be easy to demonstrate later why a body that is functioning and working to full capacity in its assigned area should in the future work on a much broader range of topics. The political goal of providing a higher level of parliamentary cooperation that can bring together, coordinate, and integrate all parliamentary functions seems to be more justifiable. This is in line with the aim of creating a common parliamentary umbrella for international cooperation that counteracts the

---

[79] A project to establish such a solution has been launched by the World Parliament Experiment in collaboration with DWB. The Global Voting Platform currently being developed is intended to enable global debates, votes, and elections on the basis of individual registrations as world citizens. See www.democracywithoutborders.org/gvp/, for a comprehensive context see Tenbergen, 2018.

[80] Cf. EP, 2008.

[81] Bummel et al., 2010.

fragmentation of the work of IPIs and the international system. A UNPA would thus be able to better address the complex interactions of the different areas and help to overcome issue silos in the UN system.

In this context, it is an instructive example that the EP from the outset served as the Joint Assembly of the three European Communities as opposed to setting up three different parliamentary bodies. In addition, it is simply not possible in practice to set up separate bodies for all the main UN institutions.

Therefore, a UNPA should, from the outset, be anchored within the international system in such a way that it has the widest possible reach and a broad thematic scope. A practical connection to the various institutions of global governance can be achieved through the work of the committees. Such a structure can be realized within the legal framework of the UN.

2.6. Establishment as a subsidiary body under Art. 22 UN Charter

A comparatively simple way to establish a UNPA would be based on a provision in the UN Charter. According to Article 22, the General Assembly may "establish such subsidiary organs as it deems necessary for the performance of its functions." Numerous institutions and programmes, such as the UN Children's Fund (UNICEF), the UN Development Programme (UNDP), the UN Conference on Trade and Development (UNCTAD), the UN High Commissioner for Refugees (UNHCR), or the UN Environment Programme (UNEP) have been established or integrated as part of the UN system under this mechanism.

A decisive advantage of this procedure is that it initially avoids the difficult process of amending the UN Charter and can serve as a basis for a possible later development of the UNPA into a main body. A decision made by the General Assembly would be sufficient. Referral to the Security Council and its approval are not required, and there is no right of veto for individual states. The statutes of a UNPA can then enter into force immediately. There would be no need to wait for countries to ratify a UNPA set up under Article 22, whereas this can be expected for a UNPA set up in an international treaty.

The powers of the General Assembly as a framework

According to Article 22, however, a UNPA can neither be established as an independent institution under international law nor as a new UN main body. Its status as a subsidiary body of the UN General Assembly would mean that it cannot be given more competences than the General Assembly itself. However, according to Articles 9 to 22 of the Charter, its powers are broad in terms of substance. The General Assembly can deal with all political issues covered by the UN Charter, provided that they are not already dealt with by the Security Council (Article 12(1)). The broad range of issues is dealt with in six main committees: Disarmament and International Security; Economic and Financial Affairs; Social, Humanitarian, and Cultural Issues; Special Political Issues and Decolonization; Administrative and Budgetary Issues; and Legal Affairs.

Although the decisions of the General Assembly are not binding on UN member states under international law, they carry political weight because they express broadly shared views among states. However, the work of the General Assembly is not only important for specific political situations. The work of the plenary and its affiliated institutions and programmes has created a framework that plays a crucial role in setting international legal norms and drafting intergovernmental treaties, including agreements such as the Framework Convention on Climate Change adopted in Rio de Janeiro in 1992.

Major tasks of the assembly include the review and approval of the UN budget and the determination of the contribution quotas of member states. The body is also involved in important elections - it appoints the UN Secretary-General on recommendation of the UN Security Council and elects the non-permanent members of the Security Council and other main UN bodies.

The most important link between the General Assembly and numerous specialized agencies and programmes of the UN system is the Economic and Social Council (ECOSOC), another main organ of the world organization. ECOSOC has a wide range of substantive working possibilities and has developed into a platform within the UN for discussing strategies for sustainable policies that are in the interests of all humanity. International civil society is also involved in this process. At present some 3,200 NGOs have consultative status with ECOSOC, which enables them to cooperate with the UN.

With regard to a UNPA, the Economic and Social Council would represent a central reference point within the world organization. However, an affiliation to ECOSOC instead of the General Assembly does not seem advisable. Apart from thematic limitations, the greater distance to the more important decision-making level of the General Assembly, to which the Council is subordinate according to Article 62 of the UN Charter, should be taken into account. The establishment as a subsidiary body of the General Assembly under Article 22 promises a much stronger and more visible position. Moreover, within this framework, the UNPA can also deal with matters that are not on the agenda of ECOSOC.

Requirements and possibilities

Having the status of a subsidiary body of the General Assembly, a parliamentary assembly would be subject to the provisions of the UN Charter, which provides guidelines for its structure and functions. In view of the principle of a universal membership of "all [...] peace-loving states" (Article 4), which is fundamental for the world organization, it can also be assumed that delegates of all UN member states would be allowed to be represented in a UNPA. However, as in the case of the Human Rights Council, certain minimum criteria could be specified.

Another fundamental provision, which a UNPA established as a subsidiary body would also be bound to, is contained in Article 2, para. 7 of the UN Charter. According to this article, the UN is not authorized to intervene in "matters which are essentially within the domestic jurisdiction of any state". A further reservation arises from Article 12, according to which the UNPA could not make recommendations on situations if the Security Council is dealing with them and the Council has not requested the assembly to do so.

Apart from such requirements, the applicability of the Charter would also entail a strengthening of the authority of the UNPA, which would thus be directly committed to the goals mentioned in the preamble. Elected representatives from all over the world would be called upon to contribute to the liberation of humanity from the "scourge of war", to respect fundamental human rights and the dignity of the human being, to uphold justice and the rule of law, and to "promote social progress and better standards of life in larger freedom".[82]

The creation of a Parliamentary Assembly as a subsidiary body of the General Assembly opens up a number of possibilities which, in our view, suggest prioritising this path of implementation over possible alternatives. First of all, it is important that the status as a subsidiary body of the UN, contrary to what the term may suggest, allows a high degree of autonomy. As a glance at the above-mentioned subsidiary bodies of the General Assembly makes clear, they have a distinctly independent profile, deal with a wide range of tasks, and are largely autonomous in the fulfilment of their functions. A UNPA would also be able to take on numerous tasks that go beyond advisory and auxiliary services. The degree of independence, which is indispensable for enabling parliamentary work, appears to be guaranteed on the basis of this legal status.

A UNPA created under Article 22 would be able to support and complement the General Assembly in the fulfilment of its tasks in many ways, while

---

[82] Preamble of the UN Charter.

also setting its own substantive priorities on the basis of parliamentary deliberations and the work of committees. Similar to the functions of other IPIs, a UNPA could exercise overarching political oversight functions over the UN system. The body would also be able to contribute to a better coordination of the work of the world organization including its various bodies and programmes and, moreover, to network with national parliaments, civil society organizations and, finally, with the world population.

Through its central integration into the organizational structure of the UN, the assembly would be provided with the foundation to act as a new important hub of global governance. The possibility of continuous substantive work on all relevant global problem areas is thus established. The annual sessions of the General Assembly also represent a good framework for the further development of the UNPA. Up to a certain point, new competences and tasks can be transferred by decisions of the General Assembly within the framework of the statutes or by amending them. Majority requirements for this, however, should not be too strict.

There are also far-reaching development prospects beyond the UN system. For instance, extending the parliamentary advisory functions of the UNPA to the economic and financial institutions such as the World Bank, IMF and WTO, would be possible by concluding respective cooperation agreements. Even before that, the UNPA could establish specialized committees that deal with global financial and trade issues. Through a fundamental reform of the UN in the course of a charter amendment, as mentioned earlier in this chapter, the assembly could eventually obtain the status of a main body. As the representation of the world's population, this parliamentary organ would then be able to interact with the General Assembly as representation of the governments of the member states in decision-making processes that deal with global challenges.

A mandate of the General Assembly

The proposed approach of establishing a UNPA under Article 22 as a subsidiary body is necessarily based on the assumption that at a certain point in time it will be possible to rely on the support of a majority of UN member states. Similar to the case of the ICC, which was established by an international treaty, this would require an international discussion and collaboration process involving the UN and its member states, the UN Commission on International Law and other experts as well as civil society.

A decision of the General Assembly will be necessary to mandate negotiations on the statutes of a UNPA under the umbrella of the UN. Based on the mandate of the General Assembly, proposals for the statutes can be drawn up within the framework of an intergovernmental negotiation process, and should only be put on the agenda of a final round of negotiations if a sufficient majority can be identified with regard to the most important elements.

The majority requirement

We assume that a UNPA can be created on the basis of a simple majority vote in the General Assembly. However, there is the possibility that the assembly might decide on the basis of Article 18 of the Charter that this is an "important question" which requires a two-thirds majority. Such a decision would itself be taken by a simple majority under paragraph 3.

We consider this to be a matter of discretion. Since the establishment of previous UN subsidiary bodies was largely by consensus, these cases cannot be used as precedents.[83] A decision by consensus is unlikely and not necessarily desirable with regard to a UNPA, since the statutes regulate complex issues and matters such as the rule of law and democratic principles have to be addressed.

The Charter also leaves room for interpretation. Among the important issues mentioned in Article 18.2, which require a two-thirds majority, the establishment of new UN bodies is not listed. However, "budgetary questions" are mentioned, which indirectly affects a UNPA if the assembly is to be financed from the UN budget.

However, this does not necessarily mean that a two-thirds majority is necessary. The General Assembly can decide on the establishment of a UNPA and its later budget in separate voting processes. Such a separation is even logical if the intention is to finance the UNPA partly or entirely outside the regular UN budget. Thus, there is no compelling reason to make a qualified two-thirds majority a prerequisite for the establishment of the UNPA.

2.7. A UN Parliamentary Network and parliamentary committees

In addition to the cooperation of the UN with the IPU, further proposals have been made for the development of a "parliamentary dimension" of the UN, which are initially below the threshold of a UNPA.

In February 2004, the report of the World Commission on the Social Dimension of Globalisation set up by the International Labour Organization

---

[83] Falk & Strauss, 2011, p. 91f.

(ILO) recommended that "parliamentary oversight of the multilateral system" at the global level should be "progressively expanded".[84] To this end, it called for the establishment of a "Global Parliamentary Group" to develop "integrated oversight" of the main institutions of the UN system, the Bretton Woods Institutions and the WTO.[85]

In its report of June 2004, the Cardoso Panel proposed that global parliamentary technical committees should be established under the aegis of the UN Secretariat and in cooperation with the IPU to discuss key global issues. These committees should consist of a geographically representative selection of members of up to thirty parliaments, each of which would belong to corresponding national parliamentary committees. Meetings should last three to four days and include experts from civil society, academia, business and other sectors. The Global Public Policy Committees would adopt reports and recommendations and become more formalized over time.[86] It was also proposed that a liaison office for parliamentary relations be established within the UN Secretariat.

A resolution adopted by PACE[87] in 2006 stated that "parliamentary involvement in the work of the UN should be enhanced progressively" going beyond cooperation with the IPU. As a first step, it recommended "the establishment of an experimental parliamentary committee with consultative functions for General Assembly committees". This should be composed of delegations elected by the national parliaments, ensuring fair geographical representation, adequate representation of the political parties represented in each parliament and gender equality. "Should this experiment be successful", it was said, "the structure and functioning of this committee could inspire the establishment of a UN parliamentary assembly with consultative functions for the plenary General Assembly."

Finally, the Commission on Global Security, Justice & Governance, co-chaired by Madeleine Albright and Ibrahim Gambari, recommended the establishment of a UN Parliamentary Network (UNPN) in 2015. The report notes that, as part of a "pragmatic approach toward strengthening UN-citizen relations and overcoming the world body's democratic deficit, a United Nations Parliamentary Network established under UN Charter Article 22 could

---

[84]   ILO, 2004, p. xiv.
[85]   Ibid., para. 544.
[86]   UN, 2004, para. 106-113.
[87]   PACE, 2006.

wield tremendous potential for expanding public knowledge of and participation in the work of the preeminent global institution".[88] The network
should be structured in a similar way to the Parliamentary Network of the
World Bank and the IMF or the Parliamentary Conference on the WTO, but
should have a "formal relationship" with the UN. The main difference to a
UNPA could therefore be that membership in the network would be open to
individual parliamentarians without the need for them to be formally elected
by their parliament or parliamentary group.[89]

In further developing the UN's "parliamentary dimension", attention
must be paid to ensuring that, in view of limited resources and capacities,
added value is always created and duplication of activities, tasks and functions
is avoided. In this respect, it should be noted that the UN already cooperates
with a number of IPIs beyond the IPU.[90] In addition, the IPU has significantly
strengthened its committee dealing with UN issues as well as its cooperation
with the UN core organization and various UN institutions over the past 15
years.[91] As far as the substantive engagement of parliamentarians with global
issues is concerned, it could be argued that this has to a certain extent been
made possible and facilitated by existing global arrangements.

The added value of the above-mentioned recommendations seems to be
that even stronger and even broader subject-related parliamentary connections with the institutions of the UN system are pursued and that these are at
least in part explicitly understood as possible preliminary stages to the development of a UNPA. In any case, the existing arrangements of the "parliamentary dimension" of the UN do not, or only to a very limited extent, perform
the role of parliamentary oversight and control vis-à-vis the UN. In this respect the status quo is minimalist and unsatisfactory.

Depending on their concrete form, the proposals of the ILO World Commission, the Cardoso Panel, PACE or the Albright-Gambari Commission
could represent useful preliminary steps. In fact, the various approaches can
be easily integrated into a new proposal. The committee proposed by PACE,
for example, could serve as the institutional umbrella for the separate committees advocated by Cardoso, which, in the spirit of the ILO report, could
also deal with the international financial institutions and the WTO and, in
the manner of a network, be open to individual members of parliament at
their own discretion.

---

[88] Commission on Global Security, Justice & Governance, 2015, pp. 84.
[89] See also Stimson Center, 2020, pp. 42-43.
[90] UN, 2018b.
[91] Bummel, 2019.

A UNPN as an intermediate step

Should a broad global discussion of the proposal for a UNPA show that for many governments the leap from the status quo to a UN body with real supervisory and monitoring rights still seems too big, the institutionalization of a parliamentary platform below this threshold could represent a feasible political compromise and a useful intermediate step.

The Albright Gambari Commission's proposal for a UNPN is considered particularly promising. On the one hand, the membership is rather informal in nature compared to the UNPA, which should lower the threshold for governments to accept it. On the other hand, such an organizational framework would also build a bridge to individual engagement of members of parliament and integrate a new energy for reforms into the UN.

However, in order to be able to lay actual solid foundations for a UNPA, a UNPN must be designed accordingly. For example, it would have to be clearly specified that the thematic focus of the body would lie on UN activities and structures in order to avoid too much overlap with existing IPIs. Above all, however, the UNPN should be clearly anchored as a precursor of a UNPA and, among other things, be entrusted with the task of dealing with the preconditions of its own transformation into a UNPA.

Although further development would ultimately remain in the hands of UN member states, the members of parliament working together in a UNPN could play a central role. There would be no need to wait for action from governments or parliaments. Interested parliamentarians could join such a network individually or in groups and set their own priorities within the framework of the overarching political objectives. It is true that the Albright Gambari Report proposes that the UNPN should be recognized by the UN General Assembly under Article 22. This would be the ideal case, but it is not an obligatory prerequisite. Other IPIs of this kind were also initially launched without official recognition of an intergovernmental organization. As soon as the UNPN reaches a sufficient size, representativeness and acceptance, a closer connection to the UN will seem logical. Ultimately, the UNPN should be transformed into a UNPA by a decision of the General Assembly.

2.8. Establishment by an intergovernmental treaty

A parliamentary assembly with a global mandate could be created within or outside the UN system by an international treaty between a group of states. In this case, cooperation agreements would regulate the functions of the body for the UN and other international institutions. A parliamentary assembly coming into existence in this way would thus not be limited to the status of a subsidiary UN organ, but could take on overarching tasks from the outset. Such a body may also be described as a Global Parliamentary Assembly (GPA), a term emphasizing that it is not only supposed to be affiliated with the core UN organization. It could inter alia provide "democratic oversight over the World Bank, the IMF and the WTO" as Boutros Boutros-Ghali demanded.[92]

The establishment of international institutions by international treaties is a routine process by means of which institutions like the IMF, the World Bank, the WTO, and the WHO were created. The example of the International Criminal Court (ICC) is particularly interesting in this context. Although the ICC is not part of the UN, crucial articles of its statute link its work to the UN Security Council, which can refer a case to the Court regardless of other jurisdictional requirements.

The emergence of the ICC is also noteworthy with regard to a UNPA. Its creation and rapid ratification by a sufficient number of states would not have been possible without the dedication of an international coalition of civil society groups. This success exemplifies that international legal structures can be established with the support of a determined group of NGOs and governments, even if political heavyweights cannot be convinced at first.[93]

More flexible options with respect to institutional design

One advantage of creating a UNPA by an intergovernmental treaty is that on this basis, a group of states can start on its own, whereas an approach within the framework of the UN requires decisions by the General Assembly and possibly other UN bodies, such as the Security Council. An additional advantage may be that higher standards in terms of both the powers to be transferred and the democratic legitimacy could be realized from the outset, if the treaty were negotiated by a smaller group of ambitious states. Thereby, the observance of human rights and the direct election of UNPA delegates could be stipulated as criteria for participation from the outset, conferring a high degree of legitimacy to the assembly and its decisions. Furthermore, the state parties could endow the body with substantial rights regarding the regulation of common tasks, including legislative powers, for instance in cooperation with national parliaments.

---

[92] Boutros-Ghali, 2007.
[93] As of 01/01/2020, 122 states have ratified the ICC Statute, excluding in particular the US, China, Russia, and India.

The problem of exclusivity

A fundamental problem of this ambitious approach is the conflict between the parliamentary assembly's global aspiration and the initially limited scope of the signatory states. The claim to speak for humanity and world society as a whole cannot credibly be made by an exclusive body that does not even have the approval of a majority of UN member states. Moreover, it seems inevitable to formally affiliate the UNPA to the UN and ideally also to other intergovernmental global governance institutions, such as the IMF, the WTO or the World Bank, in order to exert effective political influence on existing global negotiations and decision-making processes, especially with regard to participatory, supervisory, and advisory functions.

Obtaining a majority of votes at the UN to establish these links would presumably be all the more difficult, the smaller the initial number of states and the more power were supposed to be conferred to the body. A similar lack of support is to be expected in case of a commitment to the direct election of UNPA delegates, which would probably not be endorsed by many states in the beginning.

Hence, such an exclusive assembly would likely consist of an association of self-selected democracies, as has been proposed since 1939,[94] but not constitute a truly global parliament. Conversely, the ambitious long-term goal of a democratization of all states would become a precondition for a global impact of the assembly. However, the process of opening and democratizing the UN and the system of global governance must begin long before the achievement of this objective.

A pragmatic and open approach

If the aim is to achieve the greatest possible extent of global acceptance, legitimation, and functionality, a less ambitious approach regarding both access requirements and competences seems necessary in the initial phase. The high number of IPIs with limited rights of consultation, supervision, and participation created at different international institutions suggests that a comparable restriction of competences and functions may also need to be envisaged for a treaty-based UNPA with global responsibilities in order to obtain widespread approval among governments.

---

[94]   Cf. Streit, 1939; regarding an assembly of 20-30 states see Falk & Strauss, 2011, p. 95.

This approach includes the option of a group of like-minded states, which is not representing a majority at first, setting up a global parliamentary assembly outside of the UN by means of a corresponding international treaty that is open to all UN member states.[95] This step may be taken based on the consideration that the reality of such a partial assembly - and its public visibility - could in itself provide a foundation for a further global discussion of this approach and for a speedy ratification process. Once the support of a majority of governments has been achieved, the assembly could be integrated into the UN through a cooperation agreement or through the provisions of Article 22.

Approval of the UN is indispensable

From the above, the conclusion can be drawn that essentially the same conditions apply to both the creation and institutional design of a UNPA whether established by an international treaty or by a decision of the General Assembly under Article 22 of the Charter. In both cases, the approval of the UN and the participation of a majority of its member states is ultimately necessary. Consequently, the UN can and should play a major role from the outset.

The ICC may serve as an example. In this case, a preparatory process was established by the UN General Assembly, which laid the programmatic groundwork and gauged international support for the project several years prior to the ICC's founding conference in Rome in 1998. This provided the basis for the conference's success, which was held at the invitation of the UN: out of the states participating in the final vote, 120 voted yes, only seven voted no, and 21 abstained. After the deposition of the 60th instrument of ratification, the Court was able to take on its duties on July 1st 2002.

Similarly, the UN could be mandated to organize the preparatory process towards establishing a global parliamentary assembly. Once the necessary majority for this step is obtained in the General Assembly, concrete measures could be taken to negotiate its statutes within the framework of the UN.[96] The question of how to realize a UNPA under international law does not have to be decided in advance, but would be the subject of these negotiations.

The establishment of a UNPA by an international treaty offers significantly more leeway regarding its institutional design than the creation under Article 22 and allows its affiliation with the UN as well, in this case via a co-

---

[95] See the discussion of a "World Parliamentary Assembly" in Lopez-Claros et al., 2020, p. 113ff.

[96] Lopez-Claros et al., 2020 take the view that initial negotiations could also take place outside of the UN. See ibid., p. 114. In any case, the formation of a Group of Friends by progressive member states could pave the way.

Table 2: Possible forms of a global parliamentary assembly. The lines between them are fluid and often the terms are used synonymously.

Designation	Creation	Status	Selection of members	Competence
UN Parliamentary Network (UNPN)	Initiative led by MPs	Recognized by the UN, possibly based on Art. 22 UN Charter	Individual MPs at their own discretion	Advisory, possibly supervisory functions
UN Parliamentary Assembly (UNPA)	UN General Assembly in line with Art. 22 UN Charter	Subsidiary of UN General Assembly and subsequent recognised by other institutions	Through parliaments or direct vote (hybrid)	Advisory and supervisory functions, later co-decision
Global Parliamentary Assembly (GPA)	Intergovernmental treaty	Recognised by the UN and other international institutions	Through parliaments or direct vote (hybrid)	Advisory and supervisory functions, later co-decision
World Parliament (WP)	Charter reform in line with Art. 109 UN Charter	Main body of a renewed UN	Direct vote	Co-decision, law-making, supervisory functions

operation agreement. This may be the most suitable approach if there is widespread support for a global parliamentary assembly endowed with substantial rights and competences among UN members, but not enough to exceed the threshold for a charter amendment. However, if such support is limited, Article 22 seems preferable.

2.9. Conclusions

We recommend a multi-pronged political strategy for the creation of a UNPA that is primarily geared towards establishing the assembly as a subsidiary body of the UN General Assembly under Article 22 of the Charter, but continuously evaluates alternative approaches. We particularly consider the possibilities of an international treaty or a UNPN - as a preliminary stage for a parliamentary assembly - as viable options. Furthermore, in a favourable global political environment, the establishment of a UNPA as a main body of a reformed world organization by an amendment of the UN Charter should be put on the agenda. We regard a UNPA that is created below the threshold of a Charter amendment as an intermediate step towards this goal.

In our view, the primary political objective in the efforts for the establishment of a UNPA consists in initiating an inclusive and transparent process of consultations and negotiations under the auspices of the UN that involves governments, international institutions, parliamentarians, experts, representatives of civil society and citizens. Launching this process requires the political support of a majority of UN member states and a mandate of the UN General Assembly. We think that it is expedient to decide on the best procedure under international law to create the UNPA in the course of these negotiations, as the assessment of different approaches may vary depending on the political conditions, and cannot be pre-judged.

3. The UNPA as a driver of democracy

3.1. The inclusion of states with non-democratic governments

In setting up a UNPA there is a tension between the principles of universalism and democracy. On the one hand, a UNPA represents a step towards implementing more effective and accountable global governance to tackle the existential global challenges of humanity. On the other hand, the assembly is supposed to be a genuine democratic body that represents humanity in a legitimate way. The problem is that not all UN member states are democratic and allow for free and fair elections.

The model advocated so far envisages an assembly that is open to all member and observer states of the UN.[97] This concept of an assembly accessible to all states regardless of their form of government is in line with the principle of sovereign equality of UN member states in the world organization and its bodies. If a UNPA is established as a subsidiary body of the General Assembly on the basis of the UN Charter, it would likely have to satisfy this premise in principle.

A truly global approach would support the claim that a UNPA represents and speaks for humanity as a whole. Its realization requires the inclusion of representatives from states whose governments are authoritarian and oppressive, even though, as we advocate, the UNPA itself should be committed to democracy and human rights. The participation of pseudo-parliamentarians who answer to autocratic governments, however, may undermine the legitimacy and effectiveness of a UNPA.

This raises the question whether it is appropriate and feasible to limit participation to those states that meet certain minimum standards regarding the democratic legitimacy of their UNPA delegates. For the sake of the credibility of a UNPA, it may be argued that its members must be actual parliamentarians elected either by the people or by a democratically established parliament.

Furthermore, the universalist orientation of the inclusive UNPA concept developed in the 1990s reflects its historical context, and may be questioned

---

[97] CUNPA, 2007b; see also Heinrich, 2010, esp. p. 25. Thus, the only condition for access demanded is the existence of a parliament, "however this is constituted" (Bummel, 2010b, p. 30). On observer states see CUNPA, 2013, point 7.

from today's perspective. The unprecedented wave of democratization at the time led many to believe that UNPA representatives without democratic legitimacy would be more a theoretical contradiction than a problem in practice - not least since their number among the delegates would dwindle over time.[98] These ideas need to be critically re-examined considering the erosion of democracy and the rule of law in many states of the world that set in shortly after the turn of the millennium. In any case, it is highly likely that anti-democratic, reactionary, and nationalist forces will seek to organize themselves in a UNPA and use this global platform as a vehicle.

Restricting a UNPA to delegates from states with democratic governments would have the advantage of ensuring a widely shared basis of democratic values and legitimation. Such an assembly would be firmly anchored in fundamental human rights and freedoms and likely develop a corresponding reputation in the world. However, the establishment of this model also comes at a price. An assembly with restricted membership would have only limited relevance for the foreseeable future as it would only be a parliament of self-selected democracies. The claim of global representation and responsibility as well as the feasibility of organizational integration into the UN system would be jeopardized. An exclusive UNPA could therefore be less effective in addressing the global challenges of our time.

The issue of the representation of states with autocratic governments in a UNPA has been an important topic in recent years, both in the public discussion of the proposal and within the international campaign. The question was raised whether the criterion of global inclusivity should be upheld or abandoned in favour of democratic standards. Good arguments can be put forward for either approach. Both can be realized, albeit probably not in the same manner. After a brief overview of the current political status quo, we will take a closer look at the implications of both potential approaches.

3.2. The share of democratic systems in the world

Determining the ratio between democratic and non-democratic states in the world is not straightforward since there is a large variety of shades on the spectrum between the poles of democracy and despotism. However, by means of certain criteria, such as indicators relating to the rule of law, varying degrees of political freedom can be identified and countries classified accordingly.[99] Among the most renowned periodic studies of this kind are those by

---

[98] Heinrich, 2010, p. 25.
[99] On the state of democracy in the world cf. also regular blogs at www.democracywithoutborders.org/blog/.

Freedom House, the Polity Project, V-Dem, International IDEA and the classifications of the Economist Intelligence Unit.

According to Freedom House, based in Washington, D.C. that has been conducting annual surveys on the state of democracy and civil liberties around the world since the 1950s, democratic systems continue to represent the majority in the world. In 2018, 114 out of 195 states were classified as "electoral democracies", which amounts to almost 60 percent. The criteria for this category are an overall free and fair election process as well as a minimum standard of political rights and civil liberties[100]

The number of democracies identified by Freedom House has hardly changed since the turn of the millennium, yet there had been a marked increase in the number of democracies from 69 in 1989 to 120 in 1999 in the decade following the end of the Cold War.

The grey area between liberal and authoritarian systems is illustrated by a second classification applied by Freedom House. 88 out of 195 states were considered as "free" in 2018 which includes the vast majority but not all of the electoral democracies. This category encompasses 45 percent of states and 39 percent of the world population. 58 states were classified as partially free (30 percent and 24 percent of the population, respectively). 49 countries (25 percent) were considered not free - affecting 37 percent of the people in the world, half of whom live in a single country, China. The situation does not appear to have changed much since the turn of the millennium either. At the end of 1999, 85 out of 192 countries were classified as free, 59 as partially free, and 48 as not free.[101]

However, this classification does not reveal the erosion of global freedom that has been evident for years and which can be observed in terms of democratic and constitutional values, such as fair elections, freedom of the press, minority rights, the rule of law, and the separation of powers. According to Freedom House analysts, the global downward trend in this regard began in 2006 and has persisted ever since. Between 2006 and 2018, 113 countries saw a decline in the level of political and social freedom and only 63 saw an improvement. As of 2018, this trend has shown no sign of alleviation, with a ratio of 71 to 35.

This regression is also reflected in the annual Democracy Index of the Economist Intelligence Unit. According to its four-level classification, 28 out of the 167 states examined in 2006 were classified as full democracies, 54 as

---

[100]   Freedom House, 2019. They have applied stricter criteria since the status report for 2018, which led to a
        lower rating for seven states.
[101]   Freedom House, 2000.

flawed democracies, 30 as hybrid regimes and 55 as authoritarian regimes.[102] By 2019, the number of full democracies had decreased to 22, while the share of flawed democracies remained at 54 and the count of hybrid regimes increased to 37. However, the number of countries under authoritarian rule has slightly declined to 54.[103] According to the conclusions of V-Dem, democracy is still prevailing worldwide but autocratic tendencies are on the rise.[104]

These findings suggest that the trend of global democratization has not only been halted but could be reversing. The underlying problem so far is not so much the establishment of new totalitarian regimes - their number has remained more or less the same since 2006 - but rather the creeping erosion of political freedom that affects many countries worldwide, including long-established democracies. A particular point of concern is the wave of populism that has swept across the globe. Its proponents have been able to repeatedly overcome democratic protections by democratic means: namely through free elections, followed by the undermining of justice, freedom of the press, and political culture. Furthermore, various governments increasingly exert their influence to advance their anti-liberal and anti-multilateral ideologies abroad.

As mentioned in the first chapter, international surveys nonetheless indicate that the overwhelming majority of people in all regions of the world continue to support democracy as the best form of government. Compared to the 1990s, when the UNPA concept was developed, the situation is more complex and difficult today but by no means discouraging. In a UNPA open to all UN member states, parliamentarians from democracies would continue to constitute the majority according to the models presented in this policy review. An assembly based on stricter democratic standards thus would still be able to include the majority of states in the world. However, even states with anti-democratic governments often have a democratically-minded parliamentary opposition. Therefore, it cannot be assumed that the individual delegates from "non-democratic states" would all be pseudo-parliamentarians servile to their regimes. In the spirit of democracy promotion, it may therefore be seen as important to include precisely these states and to give their opposition a chance to be represented and to voice their views in a UNPA. This may be an important contribution to defending and supporting democracy.

However, societal disputes, such as attacks on the rule of law, democratic and cosmopolitan value systems, would very likely reach a global parliamen-

---

[102] Economist Intelligence Unit, 2006.
[103] Economist Intelligence Unit, 2020.
[104] V-Dem Institute, 2019.

tary assembly as well. Populists, nationalists, and autocrats would seek to organize themselves in this context in order to achieve their objectives. This does not constitute an argument against the establishment of a UNPA though. Quite the contrary. The parliamentary assembly creates a new, globally visible forum where the debate with opponents of democracy and the rule of law can be conducted freely and publicly. In this way, the international public can recognize more clearly what is at stake and new forces can be mobilized to defend and promote these values all over the world. As long as the enemies of a liberal and cosmopolitan value system do not prevail worldwide, a parliamentary chamber explicitly committed to these principles could be one of the most valuable allies to its defenders.

3.3. A parliamentary assembly on the basis of democratic standards

The arguments against including delegates from states without a democratic system of government are linked to the specific nature of a transnational parliamentary assembly. Such an institution needs to be qualitatively different from the existing intergovernmental UN organizations and international deliberative and working bodies. As a matter of principle, parliamentary work is based on the legitimacy of all representatives, conferred by citizens through free elections. Delegates who were neither elected by the people nor by a national parliament established according to democratic criteria would therefore not qualify as parliamentarians.

The participation of such delegates could undermine the legitimacy and moral authority of the assembly. Their involvement may be seen not only as a fundamental normative contradiction but also as a considerable practical problem. These delegates would be suspected of following the instructions of their governments instead of being able to make decisions freely according to the facts and their conscience. It may also be assumed that this group would be predominantly unsympathetic or even hostile towards the principles of parliamentarianism and the rule of law. The latter is particularly problematic because the UNPA would not only deal with questions of security, economy, and ecology but also with socio-political issues, such as advancing fundamental human rights and civil liberties or promoting the goals of the Agenda 2030.

An assembly that is utilized by a substantial number of pseudo-parliamentarians to fight against its very core values, including the objective of global parliamentarism itself, could lose its reputation and fall short of the expectation to serve as an engine of positive global change.

Still, even in the case of an assembly based on democratic criteria of legitimation, political compromise seems inevitable. If the requirements regarding states' democratic and constitutional standards are too demanding, the circle of participants would remain rather small. Either way, complex and probably often controversial considerations would be necessary to assess which states satisfy the requisite criteria and which fail to meet them. In order to minimize the associated potential for conflict and the possibilities of political abuse of such assessments, it is indispensable to define criteria that are universal, clear, and easy to apply. They would also have to be broad enough to enable participation beyond just a handful of model democracies.

One conceivable approach consists in focusing on the quality of elections. In accordance with certain minimum democratic standards, the representatives sent by a given country would thus have to be elected by popular vote or by a directly elected national parliament.

Delegates from states that do not meet these criteria could be allowed to participate in the deliberations and the work of the assembly as observers but be barred from voting. By means of this arrangement, it would theoretically be possible to achieve global inclusiveness while upholding minimum democratic requirements for the parliamentary assembly. However, it is unlikely that states affected by this restriction would approve of this procedure. Instead, they might accuse the institution of discrimination and exclusion. After all, a participation without the right to vote is tantamount to acknowledging a regime's underlying lack of basic democratic legitimacy.

The necessity of minimum democratic standards for the election of UNPA delegates would require corresponding provisions in the statutes or rules of procedure of the assembly. The criteria must directly relate to the parliamentary systems of member states: Where delegates are appointed by national parliaments, the members of those parliaments must themselves have received sufficient democratic legitimacy through a popular vote. Where delegates are directly elected, a free and fair election procedure must be guaranteed. In addition, it needs to be ensured that the delegates sent to the UNPA adequately reflect the political spectrum that exists in each country.[105]

A minimum requirement for assessing a state's electoral system can be derived from Article 21(3) of the UDHR, which stipulates that the will of the people "shall be expressed in periodic and genuine elections which shall be by universal and equal suffrage and shall be held by secret vote or by equivalent free voting procedures". Political competition within a multi-party system is

---

[105] This speaks in favor of a system of proportional representation.

essential in this context. Accordingly, cases of blatant electoral fraud are just as unacceptable as one-party systems in democratic disguise, in which the population can de facto at most choose between candidates who have been approved by the government.

Establishing such guidelines is certainly possible, and participating states could be expected to be willing and able to implement and comply with these rules. An electoral commission appointed by the assembly or the plenary could monitor compliance with the required standards.

Under the regulations outlined above, countries not permitted to send delegates would include civil war zones, so-called failed states, absolute monarchies, one-party systems, military dictatorships and dependent regions. In addition, they would rule out countries in which elections have been delayed for a long period of time, where massive electoral fraud has been observed or where no political competition between parties can take place.[106] However, so-called electoral autocracies, in which political systems with limited democratic standards are confirmed by the population through generally fair elections, would still belong to the circle of participants.

It is worth noting that the guidelines presented here leave room for a "backdoor". Even for unambiguously undemocratic states, in which no parliamentary opposition exists, membership seems possible in principle, if at least a free and fair election of the UNPA delegates by their population is guaranteed. Nevertheless, this scenario is obviously highly unlikely.

Establishment as an independent institution under international law

Deciding on a parliamentary assembly whose participating states must meet democratic criteria could impede its establishment as a subsidiary body of the UN General Assembly under Article 22 of the Charter. According to the Charter, the political order of a state is irrelevant for its membership in the UN. As this rule hitherto applies to all the UN bodies, it could be argued that under international law, restricting a country's access to a UNPA would contradict the principle of sovereign equality of all states.

However, the rules of procedure of the UN Human Rights Council, established in 2006 as a subsidiary body of the General Assembly, support the assumption that there may be exceptions to this rule. According to the founding resolution, the General Assembly, "by a two-thirds majority of the members present and voting, may suspend the rights of membership in the Council of

---

[106]   According to these criteria, countries such as Saudi Arabia and China could not send delegates to a UNPA.

a member of the Council that commits gross and systematic violations of human rights".[107] Nevertheless, this does not constitute a general access restriction based on general human rights standards, as increasingly demanded. The UN Human Rights Council is often criticized precisely because of the continuous membership of states in which the most serious human rights violations are being committed.

Instead of applying Article 22, it would be more expedient to create a parliamentary assembly on the basis of minimum democratic standards as an independent institution under international law by means of an intergovernmental treaty and then link the assembly to the UN via a cooperation agreement. This approach enables a UNPA to operate without direct ties to the UN General Assembly and the UN Charter. Moreover, it permits in particular the stipulation of membership obligations including the transfer of supranational powers. However, the integration of the assembly into the UN system requires a majority decision of the General Assembly or the main bodies of other UN institutions. Thus, the approval of a majority of states in the world is still necessary after all.

If there is sufficient support in the international community, the creation of a parliamentary specialized agency at the UN could mark a significant step towards the development of global democracy. Compared to a UNPA established under Article 22, a higher level of democratic legitimation could be realized as well as more comprehensive and effective competences to fulfill global tasks - without having to forego inclusion in the UN system in principle. At the same time, the deepened political integration of a large group of states in a global parliamentary institution could be a catalyst for transformation processes in other countries and lead to a growing membership. However, building broad agreement for this path is an extraordinary political challenge that may only be met when the window of opportunity of a special historical context arises.

3.4. A parliamentary assembly with universal membership

The advantage of a universal world parliamentary assembly is that it can act as the voice of the whole human community. Through its global inclusiveness, it symbolizes the indivisibility of humanity as well as the indivisibility of the earth.[108] It embodies the ideas that global politics must be oriented towards the common good, that the basic needs of every human being on earth

---

[107] UN, 2006, point 8.
[108] Spiegel, 2009, p. 246.

must be taken into account as well as the right to personal development, and that people need to be better represented and more involved in global policy-making processes. An inclusive UNPA underpins the notion of a collective commitment to the entire planetary community.

While the exclusion of states under authoritarian rule benefits the democratic credibility of the assembly, it undermines the credibility of the global perspective that a UNPA is supposed to represent. It would be easy to present such a body as an exclusive club whose work is only in the interest of part of the international community and which therefore cannot claim to speak on behalf of humankind.

This would call into question the objective of a UNPA to bring together representatives from all states of the world to work out global solutions. Crises, such as climate change, not only affect all people in both democratic and authoritarian states, but also require cooperation of their governments according to jointly agreed and implemented rules. A UNPA which is too exclusive would forfeit its claim of being a global forum for negotiating universally valid democratic rules that serve the implementation of a fair balance of interests and the common ability to act at the global level.

Moreover, cooperation with the UN could turn out to be much more problematic if a UNPA is not based on the principle of universal membership. Firstly, it could be more difficult if not impossible to establish the body as a subsidiary organ of the General Assembly this way. Secondly, interlinking with the various UN institutions would also be more complicated, since the countries excluded from the assembly would be represented in those institutions. Furthermore, an exclusive approach challenges the perspective of refocusing global political decisions within the framework of the UN by providing the General Assembly with a consultative body which would reflect the demographic importance of states by means of a weighted distribution of seats.

This raises the question whether the disadvantages arising from the loss of the global dimension can be outweighed by the strengthening of democratic credibility. Again, political compromises are necessary if the new assembly is not just to be a small club of developed democracies. The degree to which governments guarantee political freedoms varies widely. Where should the line be drawn? Even though free elections would be a generally applicable criterion, the process of establishing standards for assessing the quality of elections entails considerable challenges with respect to weighing up different aspects. Formally largely free and fair elections may well be accompanied by massive discrimination against the opposition and severe restrictions of fundamental freedoms, a practice frequently applied by modern autocrats.

Other approaches instead of excluding states

The guiding principle of universal membership is seriously tested in a scenario where delegates from governments responsible for gross human rights violations debate the promotion of democracy and fundamental social values in the assembly. Or when countries only send delegates from the ruling government because no parliamentary opposition can be formed in their political system. Nevertheless, it should be considered whether other approaches might serve the interest of the people better than the exclusion of the states concerned.

An alternative option would be to enshrine certain safeguards in the statutes of the assembly. These include the possibility to co-opt representatives of minorities and opposition movements into committees by the parliamentary groups which would give them a right to participate and speak in the assembly. In the case of serious human rights violations, provisions should be made to suspend the voting rights of those delegates who represent those decision-makers to whom a shared responsibility can be attributed, similar to the procedure in the UN Human Rights Council.

Of special importance is the task of a UNPA to conduct public debates on violations of fundamental rights and freedoms committed in UN member states. In this way, the assembly should bring the fate of those affected to the fore and put pressure on the respective governments to justify their actions, for example by demanding that they uphold the responsibility to protect.

Receiving such criticism could lead some repressive governments to consider withdrawing their delegates from the assembly - although they would have to weigh up this decision against the public loss of reputation. The possible withdrawal of such states would increase the proportion of democratic delegates in the assembly. Thereby, the character of a universal UNPA, open to all states, would in practice shift towards an assembly based on minimum democratic standards. In this case, however, the door for the membership of all states would remain open without restriction, and the universalist claim of being the voice of humanity would be preserved.

The example of the PAP

The question of the representation of states with undemocratic systems of government is not a novel issue that only arises with regard to a UNPA. Parliamentary assemblies and regional parliaments are already confronted with this contradiction. For instance, the Parliamentary Assembly of the Council of Europe (PACE) initially comprised exclusively democracies, but since the second wave of accession of countries from Eastern Europe and the former

Soviet Union, the institution has had to cope with a much more heterogeneous composition.

The example of the Pan-African Parliament (PAP) is particularly interesting. It was established in 2004 as a consultative organ of the African Union (AU), although there are numerous authoritarian and totalitarian political systems among the 55 member states. Analogous to what the UNPA concept envisages for the global level, Article 2(2) of the founding protocol adopted in 2001 states that the PAP delegates represent "all the peoples of Africa", and Article 4 stipulates that all states of the AU are members.[109]

Noteworthy is also a provision that should similarly be applied to a UNPA as well: according to Article 4(3), the delegations sent by the member states must reflect the political spectrum of parliaments or any equivalent advisory bodies, which can only be convincingly achieved in democratic states.

Despite the very heterogeneous composition of the PAP in terms of the member countries' standards of democracy and the rule of law, Article 3 of the founding protocol explicitly refers to the delegates' obligation to promote fundamental social values, including human rights, democracy, peace, good governance, development, and cooperation. As a long-term goal for the development of the PAP, Article 2(3) states the ultimate aim "to evolve into an institution with full legislative powers, whose members are elected by universal adult suffrage".

Similarly, a UNPA open to all member states would be a first step towards bridging the divide between democratic and non-democratic states, on which a democratically legitimized world order can be built over time as democratization progresses.

The connection between legitimacy and powers

The possible negative influences arising from the participation of UNPA delegates who are closely associated with governments exhibiting democratic and rule of law-related deficits are put in perspective in the light of the body's initial powers which would be largely limited to advisory functions. The assembly has neither the mandate to intervene in national legislation nor to shape binding international regulations. At the beginning, the assembly's work would only involve accompanying global policy and its implementation - which, under the current conditions, requires states to work together to achieve common goals, in spite of their varying forms of government. In the further development of the UNPA, any transfer of substantial powers to the

---

[109]   In fact, all AU members have now ratified the relevant protocol and have become members.

body will have to be accompanied by a strengthening of its democratic legitimacy. In this sense, "direct elections of the UNPA's delegates" can be seen as a prerequisite "for vesting the body with legislative rights".[110]

Conclusion

There are good arguments for making access to a UNPA conditional on the observance of minimum democratic standards by UN member states, even if major practical problems would have to be overcome with respect to implementation. However, all things considered, we come to the conclusion that an open, inclusive and universal approach best serves the cause of a global parliamentary assembly committed to all humankind that has links to the UN and deals with global challenges. We suggest that only those few states that either have no parliament at all or a parliament indistinguishable from the executive should not be able to participate in a UNPA.[111]

3.5. Dealing with autocratic and nationalist perspectives

According to the models of seat distribution we examined, delegates from electoral democracies and proponents of pro-democratic forces from transition countries would currently constitute the majority in the assembly. None of the models showed more than a third of the seats being occupied by parliamentarians from countries classified as non-free.[112] Moreover, the latter cannot simply be lumped together; there are also pro-democratic groups in many of these countries, albeit not in all of them. These findings support the expectation that a UNPA with universal membership can work successfully as a democratic organ and in favor of global democratization.

Furthermore, there is reason to hope that the anti-democratic wave that has emerged across the world over the last ten years will abate in the foreseeable future and that a global trend towards more democracy will resume. The broad acceptance of democratic forms of government as well as of fundamental human rights and freedoms among the world's population is unwavering. This bedrock of values makes it seem likely that people will demand their fundamental right to democracy more vigorously and successfully again in the future. Another silver lining in this context is that all over the world, new movements committed to the realization of fundamental human rights and freedoms have evolved. They challenge the reactionary, exclusive, and anti-

---

[110]   CUNPA, 2007b. See also p. 86.
[111]   The remaining six absolute monarchies that are members of the UN are particularly problematic.
[112]   See the scenarios for seat allocation, ch. 5.

democratic forces and expose their inhuman ideologies. If they increasingly cooperate across national borders, they can better support each other and thereby expand their global influence. A UNPA would be able to foster, interconnect, and strengthen this endeavour in many ways.

Commitment to human rights

It could not be ruled out, indeed it is likely that various delegates in a UNPA would act on behalf of their government or as lobbyists, that they would represent specific national interests instead of the general interest, or even that they would try to use the platform committed to the values of global democracy, rule of law and transnational cooperation to dismantle those very norms. However, we believe that a UNPA can be designed in a way that its orientation and mode of operation would create very unfavourable conditions for such efforts. First of all, the founding statutes should contain an unequivocal commitment to the basic human rights principles of the UN Charter and the UDHR. The work of UNPA delegates would have to be measured against these fundamental values.

The role of parliamentary procedures

The UNPA is supposed to function as an assembly of democratically legitimized representatives of the people, who deliberate independently, decide according to facts and conscience, and are not responsible to their countries of origin or their governments, but to humanity as a whole. On the basis of the statutes, they shall have the mandate and the duty to consider the interests of the entire world society, to develop their policies from a global perspective and to promote the unity of humankind.

Against this background, it is not unlikely that delegates who advocate populist and nationalist views or authoritarian values in the UNPA will undermine their own credibility. They would have to present their arguments within the framework of parliamentary practices and procedures. Unlike government representatives in an intergovernmental body, they could not simply fall back on certain positions of their country. They would have to justify their opinions with reference to public interests and present them in a general and open debate. They would be exposed to the counter-arguments of other parliamentarians, would have to accept compromises, adapt their positions, and integrate themselves into political groups in order to advance their views in the UNPA. It is also possible that some delegates might initially join as loyal mouthpieces of their government, but over time become advocates of UNPA viewpoints in their respective home countries.[113]

Independent exercise of the mandate

Furthermore, an independent exercise of their UNPA mandate by individual delegates can be encouraged by establishing sound rules of procedure. In order to avoid obvious conflicts of interest, delegates who hold a government office or belong to a national or international civil service should not be able to be members of the UNPA at the same time. Similar requirements could be considered for those holding positions in sensitive businesses or associations.

In addition, it should be stipulated that UNPA delegates may not be removed from office before the end of their regular tenure by institutions of their country, in particular the government, parliament or their parliamentary group. If they have been duly elected and accredited, their seat must be secure for the entire term of office. National prosecution of UNPA members or any restrictions on their freedom should only be allowed with the consent of the assembly after examination by a committee of privileges and a plenary vote.

If certain votes in the assembly were to be cast in secret, it would significantly limit the ability of autocratic governments to control and sanction the voting behaviour of individual delegates. On the other hand, such a measure would have the disadvantage of impairing the transparency of parliamentary work and weakening the relation of UNPA delegates to the citizens. In this case, it would hardly be possible to hold delegates accountable for a certain voting behaviour. This may have to be decided on a case-by-case basis.

Regulations against lobbying and corruption

Reliable regulations against non-transparent lobbying and corruption should be in place. Whereas the influence of various interest groups - often via political consultancies - on the work of elected officials can in principle be considered legitimate with regard to global political processes as well, it should be disclosed to the extent possible. Similar to the regulations of the European Commission and the EP, a UNPA should create a transparency register listing all interest group representatives who want to get in touch with UNPA delegates or their staff. In this context, a code of conduct for lobbyists and parliamentarians could be established. Moreover, delegates should also be obliged

---

[113] Heinrich, 2011, p. 34.

to publish other employment and sources of income. It could also be requested that they disclose all meetings with lobbyists online, following the example of a regulation adopted by the EP in 2019.[114]

In addition to a verifiable code of conduct, other measures against corruption should include the establishment of an independent commission of inquiry affiliated to the UNPA. Such a body was temporarily set up by PACE in 2017 after allegations of bribery had been made against various members.[115] In the case of a UNPA, it could be a permanent body. Furthermore rules on campaign and political financing should be established to ensure political influence cannot be bought.

3.6. The importance of transnational groups

One structural principle key to the democratic character of the UNPA is its ability to represent the political spectrum of parliaments in the case of indirect elections and the will of the people in the case of popular elections. While the bodies of intergovernmental institutions are generally composed of delegates of the respective incumbent governments only, opposition parties are to be represented in the UNPA in addition to government parties. This will result in a voice for opposition and a broader range of political opinion.

In general, delegates of a given country belonging to different political camps will not only have distinct conceptions of fundamental objectives, but also of what is in their "national interest". Minorities may either be represented directly by parliamentarians in a UNPA or can choose to cooperate with sympathetic members and groups to contribute their views at the global level. Any attempts by delegates to claim a specific agenda to be the sole will of their nation will thus likely be seen to be unfounded.

Of crucial importance for the cosmopolitan-democratic character of the UNPA is a transnational mode of operation and culture of debate. Even though delegates with the same nationality may vote the same way in some cases, members of the assembly would be expected - and required - to form transnational political groups according to shared political beliefs and worldviews, similar to the parliamentarians in the EP or PACE, instead of organizing along the lines of national delegations. Such organizational processes can be supported and promoted by appropriate rules of procedure in a UNPA.

---

[114] EP, 2019a.
[115] Council of Europe, 2018.

The UNPA statutes should give transnational groups a central position in the processes and procedures of the assembly. These groups can receive financial support and key procedural rights similar to those in the EP, such as representation in committees or the ability to table draft resolutions. The number of seats allocated to a group in a committee should in principle depend on its share of seats in the plenary.

Requirements for the formation of groups

Compared to the EP, the delegates of a UNPA will represent a greater variety of political views, parties, and groupings, which is why the formation of more groups is to be expected. Furthermore, a high number of independent members can be anticipated. These members should not be marginalized by the suggested focus on the procedural rights of the groups. In any case, the basis for the recognition of a group should be that its members must come from a certain minimum number of states. Since 2009, the EP's rules of procedure stipulate that at least 25 members from at least a quarter of the EU member states are required to form a political group; a PACE group must include 28 delegates from eight countries.

In contrast, groups of a UNPA will have to exhibit not only a transnational, but also a global character. Their membership will thus have to include delegates from a certain number of world regions as well. In this context, member states could be divided into world regions different from the UN's current unofficial geopolitical groups (where the states of North America form a group with those of Western Europe and Australia, for example).

Furthermore, regulations for a UNPA should ensure that only groups which share a common ideological orientation and which actually work together substantively are granted the status of a group. The formation of "mixed" or "technical" groups of parties or individual delegates who seek to secure the advantages of that status without cooperating for common goals is contrary to the objective of promoting transnational work.

In the EP, such groups were initially formed several times, but a judgement by the European Court of Justice in 2001 objected to this practice. The then existing "Technical Group of Independents" had to be dissolved.[116] However, in general, the Bureau of the EP does not check whether the members of a

---

[116] European Court of Justice, 2001.

group actually have a common political orientation.[117] In the case of the technical groups though, this was very obviously lacking.[118]

Dealing with pseudo-groups

Due to the greater diversity of political views, the issue of pseudo-groups seems even more significant for a UNPA than for the EP. It might therefore be advisable that a competent body, such as the bureau or a special committee, routinely evaluates the formation of political groups and reviews them over time. In this context, it is also to be discussed whether delegates whose political intentions contradict the objectives of the UNPA should be allowed to form a group at all. For instance, should groups that have the aim of obstructing the work of the UNPA or even dissolving the assembly be permitted? Should it be possible that groups which openly oppose democratic principles and human rights operate in a UNPA? From our perspective delegates individually need to commit to these principles as well as to the statutes of the UNPA and this should apply to groups as well.

The rules of procedure of PACE[119] stipulate that newly formed political groups must be recognized by the bureau of the assembly. The members concerned shall state their common objectives and explicitly declare that they share a common ideological and political orientation. They are also required to promote and respect the values of the Council of Europe, in particular political pluralism, human rights and the rule of law[120] in their statute and activities. With reference to this provision, the planned formation of a new group of right-wing nationalists and populists called New European Democrats/Europe of Nations was rejected in 2019.[121]

If the provisions to form groups in a UNPA were subject to similar standards, this could contribute to achieving a certain degree of resilience in upholding the founding principles of this institution, even if delegates from all UN member states participate. However, eligibility must be regulated in a transparent and convincing manner in order to prevent possible abuse.

The regulations of PACE can also serve as an instructive example of how independent delegates can get involved. Irrespective of their membership in a political group, each representative should, for example, be able to propose draft resolutions. If these resolutions are supported by a certain number of

---

[117]   See Art. 30 of the EP's 2009 Rules of Procedure .
[118]   On the issue in the EP see also Leinen, 2019.
[119]   See Art. 19 of the Rules of Procedure of the Assembly of May 2019.
[120]   Ibid., Art. 19(1).
[121]   AFP, 2019.

other delegates, the bureau could decide whether to hand the draft resolution to the responsible committee for further consultation.

Global parties and transnational lists

The experience in the EU suggests that an essential role of political groups in the functioning of the UNPA will presumably lead to a stronger cooperation of ideologically related national parties within the framework of international umbrella associations and in the long run promote the emergence of global parties. It is to be expected that existing world associations and networks such as the Centrist Democrat International, Global Greens, Liberal International, Progressive Alliance or Socialist International will cooperate with like-minded groups in the UNPA. In this light, it is interesting that two world congresses of the Global Greens[122] as well as the Liberal International,[123] Pirate Parties International[124] and the Socialist International[125] have already endorsed the establishment of a UNPA.

The strengthening or establishment of global party work within and outside of a UNPA does not necessarily have to include the introduction of transnational electoral lists at first. To conduct elections within the framework of existing states has two major advantages. First, the candidates are more or less familiar with the situation in their respective countries. Second, they are known to the voters or have a realistic chance of attaining a public profile through their election campaign. For the foreseeable future, these general conditions are likely to remain basic requirements for ensuring a genuine interest of the population in global elections and for their bond to the global parliament. Finally, holding the elections within existing states is relatively easy to implement and thus represents a pragmatic and realistic approach, at least in the early stages. Transnational lists would represent a high political and technical hurdle for the establishment of a UNPA. Even for a limited number of seats in the EP, an agreement in favour of transnational lists has not yet been reached.

Differences with national parliaments

With regard to the democratic character of a UNPA, an important difference between a supranational and a national parliament should be highlighted. As

---

[122] Global Greens, 2008 and 2012.
[123] Liberal International, 2005.
[124] Pirate Parties International, 2013.
[125] Socialist International, 2003 and 2005.

the example of the EP illustrates, the former lacks a clear political confrontation between government groups and opposition parties, although dominant political groups or coalitions emerge, of course. This reduces the pressure to conform to party positions and allows greater independence and political room for manoeuvre for both delegates and political groups; parliamentarians can vote more freely according to their convictions and the facts of the situation rather than according to political agendas. The voting behaviour that can be observed in the EP confirms this expectation, as majorities often change depending on the subject of the vote. For the same reasons, developing a transnational structure for the UNPA should also allow for a detachment from political constraints, foster an independent handling of substantive issues, and benefit from an open discourse, in which the power of facts and convincing arguments should prevail.

A step towards cosmopolitan democracy

The self-organization of the elected UNPA members into institutionalized parliamentary groups represents an important concrete step towards growing an active cosmopolitan democracy. With regard to the EU, Article 10 of the Treaty on the EU underlines the importance of political parties at the European level, which contribute "to forming European political awareness and to expressing the will of citizens of the Union". A similar development can also be expected with regard to a UN Parliamentary Assembly.

Against the background of the considerations and recommendations made in this chapter, we believe it is justified to assume not only that a UNPA could function successfully according to basic democratic principles, but that it can also serve as a driving force for global democratization. This view is supported by the preponderance of democratic systems globally and by the widespread support of democratic forms of government amongst the world population. It is also underpinned by the base of moral values, the reputation, the specific nature of operations and the possibilities for political impact which can be expected from an assembly that is as democratically legitimized and representative as possible, but nevertheless universally oriented. Furthermore, if democratic standards continue to spread in the world, the democratic nature of the UNPA would become more and more deeply embedded.

4. The procedure for the election of delegates

4.1. Selection of delegates by parliaments or popular vote

The nation states as a framework

In accordance with parliamentary tradition, the members of a UNPA would have demonstrable democratic legitimacy and would have to be considered free and unbound by instructions in the exercise of their mandate.[126] As long as collective and free world elections[127] are not feasible, nation states are the most obvious framework in which democratic legitimacy is established and electoral processes take place. Three basic options are under discussion in this regard:

1. Members are elected from within national parliaments or political groups formed therein.
2. National parliaments or political groups formed therein act as electoral colleges and elect the representatives from among the entire population.
3. Members are elected directly by the citizens of the country of origin in free, secret, and equal elections.

Election by parliaments from their membership

The selection of the members of a UNPA by national parliaments represents a technically simple process that is well established in the practice of existing parliamentary assemblies. No major bureaucratic burden and corresponding costs would be involved and from the beginning, implementation would be possible in all UNPA member states according to universal rules. A variation, which we will discuss later, consists of delegates not being elected by the full parliament, but directly by respective political groups according to the number of seats allocated to each of them.

---

[126]   Cf. Heinrich 2011, p. 11.
[127]   Monbiot, 2004, p. 100.

In some countries, the legislative branch consists of two chambers, usually a directly elected chamber representing citizens[128] and another chamber representing constituent states[129]. In such cases it may be useful, in principle, if delegates to a UNPA are elected by the chamber that represents citizens. This would make the selection process easier and more in line with procedures applied in one chamber-systems. An inclusion of the chamber of the constituent states of UN member countries would complicate the procedure, but need not be ruled out. Under the condition that this serves to reflect the political forces present in the legislative branch as accurately as possible, it could be left to the participating states themselves whether and how they wish to include both chambers in the selection of their UNPA members.

In any case, this procedure is based on the assumption that the elected UNPA members will remain members of their respective parliaments. One advantage of this dual membership is the permanent link it would create between the UNPA and national parliaments. Thus, views of the individual parliaments could be integrated into the work of the global parliamentary assembly in a simple way and vice versa. Moreover, the establishment of common working levels on political issues seems to be possible in a straightforward manner. The dual mandate may also be helpful to increase the support in the nation states necessary for the further development of the assembly. The experience of being a UN parliamentarian "will galvanize many of these politicians into going home as advocates for the UN, including the need for strengthening and democratizing the UN Parliamentary Assembly itself", as Dieter Heinrich put it.[130]

However, these advantages come at the price that national parliamentarians can devote only a small share of their time to the concerns of the UNPA. Furthermore, it cannot be denied that a selection carried out by individual parliaments does not represent an ideal solution in terms of democratic theory. This method only generates an indirect legitimation by the population and results in a greater distance from the citizens. This problem may be all the more relevant with regard to countries whose parliamentary systems are weak. In any case, it would remain a constant challenge to convince the population that these parliamentary selections are relevant to them.

With regard to this electoral procedure, we propose that members of the UNPA will be elected by the political groups represented in the parliaments

---

[128]   Like the German Bundestag, the US House of Representatives or the Indian Lok Sabha (usually called the "lower house").

[129]   Like the German Bundesrat, the US Senate or the Indian Rajya Sabha (usually called the "upper house").

[130]   Heinrich, 2010, p. 24.

or alliances formed specifically for this purpose. The possible alternative of a joint election by the whole plenary of the respective parliament would have the obvious disadvantage that the ruling party could not only determine the selection of its own UNPA members, but also influence the selection of the opposition representatives. The parties or groupings should be able to act independently. In the case that a selection by parliaments from the general population would be established for UNPA members instead, the parties or associations could function as autonomous electoral colleges. In case of direct elections of delegates by the population, they would draw up the electoral lists.

Election by parliaments from among citizens

Another possibility is that parliaments elect UNPA members not from their midst, but from the ranks of the entire citizenship of their country. So far, this approach has played little role in the composition of IPIs. An exception is the legislative body of the East African Community, the East African Legislative Assembly (EALA). The members of this body are elected in this manner by the parliaments of the six member states of the Community on the condition that the respective representation of political parties is reflected in the best possible way.[131] This procedure will also be applied to the election of the members of PAP once the Malabo Protocol of 2014 receives the necessary number of ratifications.[132]

Advantages of such a procedure for a UNPA would be the possibility of a diverse representation of the respective society, of the involvement of renowned personalities from different fields, and that the selected persons could fully dedicate themselves to their duties as UNPA members. However, it also entails the necessity to pay appropriate allowances, while in the case of delegates selected from parliament membership, it can be assumed that their UNPA-related activities are largely covered by their remuneration under their national mandate. Due to the increased costs involved, the chances of realizing this approach appear comparatively low in the given political reality.

Moreover, doubts can be raised as to the democratic legitimacy and transparency of the procedure. The selection of the delegates could be too far removed from the respective political landscape of a given state, making it appear opaque and unrepresentative. In particular, the question arises as to the criteria by which the candidates would be determined and what societal po-

---

[131] See Art. 50(1), Treaty for the Establishment of the East African Community.
[132] See Art. 5.1a in African Union, 2014.

sitions would be represented in each case. The necessity of designating the delegates according to the political composition of the parliament, as provided for in terms of EALA and the Malabo Protocol, therefore appears to be an indispensable element of this election method if it were considered for a UNPA.

This method of indirect election also means that, unlike directly elected members of parliament and national parliamentarians, candidates do not have to run a public election campaign, but only need to convince the relevant parliament. They thus only enjoy limited legitimacy. At the very least there should be public hearings and multiple candidates per seat.

Should states not be able to agree on general, comprehensible and verifiable standards by which to select from among the population, there would also be a continuing uncertainty as to whether the members of the assembly actually represent the population of their country, the political currents existing there, or above all certain interests that are advocated by parties or other associations. It is a fundamental principle of parliamentarism that elections set political priorities, and this principle would be violated if such priorities were not reflected in the composition of a UNPA.

Popular elections

A direct election of UNPA members by the population in a free, fair and equal voting procedure would provide the best possible democratic legitimacy. The people's commitment to the UNPA and the perception of its activities by the public would be much stronger than in the previous procedures. Citizens in the respective countries would be called upon to make their own decisions at regular intervals. They could actively consider the candidates standing for election, reflect on global issues and political positions, and by doing so participate in a general public discourse. In this way, they would be able to elect the candidates they consider most suitable on the basis of their own political will, and they would also be able to withdraw corresponding mandates. The elected individuals would be able to dedicate their entire working time to the UNPA and to provide a variety of services on a global level. Since they would have competed specifically for this task, they could be expected to show conviction and commitment.

Special importance could be attributed to the public debates expected in the run-up to the election. While periodic elections to the UNPA in parliament would easily run the risk of being lost in the social perception as tasks among many others, a popular election would attract much broader attention. There would be political statements, public events, and media coverage. Global challenges and the UNPA's efforts to tackle them would be addressed.

The public would be sensitized to the concrete effects of globalization on the everyday life of each individual. At the same time, the impression of powerlessness with regard to these developments could be confronted.

By means of popular elections to the UNPA, the people of the world would for the first time be directly involved in decision-making at the global level and in shaping global policy. A global civic sense of responsibility and global citizenship could gain strength in the midst of societies and in its wake a stronger dynamic for change at the global level.

4.2. Parliamentary selection as a minimum condition

The direct election of UNPA delegates complies with basic parliamentary and democratic principles in the best possible way. From the point of view of democratic legitimacy and the ability of the delegates to concentrate on their global mandate, direct elections are the best foundation for assigning important functions and tasks to the assembly as well as for promoting a supportive political culture in the member states.

Nevertheless, it does not seem advisable to make direct elections a prerequisite for participation from the outset. At this point, such an ambition could drastically reduce the acceptance of the project among governments and thus its chances of realization. Governments may initially shy away from the logistical effort and cost of direct elections. For policy makers who reject a parliamentarization of the UN for ideological and other reasons, a reference to supposedly too high costs might also offer a welcome pretext to block a UNPA.

In a global political situation where, for the most part, only a limited will for change can be expected, a realistic approach that builds on well-established political practice and can be implemented immediately without major effort is of great advantage. If successful, it will also pave the way for further steps forward at a later stage.

The procedure of a parliamentary selection of delegates as a minimum condition for participation is a path that is immediately feasible for all states. However, while this excludes the simple appointment of representatives by the government executive or other non-parliamentary institutions, it does not eliminate the possibility of individual states setting higher standards on their own initiative.

The selection by parliaments corresponds to a well-established practice with regard to the composition of international parliamentary assemblies and other IPIs. Although this method does not implement the democratic standard of direct elections at the international level, it is nevertheless based on the participation of elected representatives. Frequently, the size of the population and the political weight of the participating states are taken into account, and in some instances, as in the case of PACE, the representation of political parties in the respective parliaments is considered as well. The model of a UNPA built on the example of well-developed parliamentary assemblies combines political practicability with a level of legitimacy that is sufficient for the first step. It also offers a suitable framework for a gradual transition to direct elections.

4.3. Moving toward direct elections: a two-speed UNPA

In order to move from parliamentary to direct elections, two transition strategies are conceivable. One possibility is the establishment of clearly separated stages of development with essentially the same election procedure for all states. In this case, the selection of delegates could initially be carried out by parliaments in a uniform manner, resulting in a UNPA of national parliamentarians. After a designated transitional period, direct elections could become compulsory for all member states in a second phase of development. An alternative would be that the states themselves decide within the framework of common procedural rules when they make the transition from parliamentary to direct elections, which would result in a two-speed UNPA. Finally, both approaches could also be combined by setting a deadline until which a transition to direct elections should have been made.

The example of the EP and direct elections to a UNPA

An interesting example of the first approach is how the election of the EP has evolved. The predecessor of the EP was a parliamentary assembly that was assigned as a supervisory body to the European Coal and Steel Community (ECSC) founded in 1951. With the 1958 Treaties of Rome, it became the common assembly of the three European Communities (ECSC, EEC and Euratom). The founding treaties already stipulated that the members of this body would initially be appointed by the national parliaments, but later on be determined by direct universal elections. This transition was rendered binding for all member states by an act of the Council of Ministers in 1976. The first direct election to the EP took place in 1979.

The major stride towards direct elections was followed by numerous other reform steps, which not only extended the EP's powers but also further consolidated the democratic character of the supranational elections themselves. In the Maastricht Treaty of 1992, the states agreed that the elections to the EP must follow a uniform procedure. In 2002, in addition to the principle of proportional representation, the incompatibility of national and European mandates was established, thus ensuring that all MEPs are able to concentrate fully on their work at the European level. Finally, the 2009 Treaty of Lisbon made EP elections a fundamental right of the European Union with the requirement of a "direct universal suffrage in a free and secret ballot".[133]

However, the assumption of a comparable development of the election process to a UNPA presents a number of problems. In the European Community, the decision to introduce direct elections had to be based on an unanimous decision of the Council of Ministers, which only came about after 18 years of continuous political struggle. At that time, the EEC had only nine member states after the first enlargement. At the world level, however, both a much larger number of states and a much greater diversity of political systems must be taken into account. If the establishment of a general consensus among governments were to be made a prerequisite for a general and simultaneous introduction of direct elections, it could be expected that a UNPA would be cemented as an assembly of national parliamentarians for the foreseeable future, and its further democratic development would be blocked.

The path via a qualified majority decision of the state parties or the UNPA itself, if binding on the minority, is no more promising. Doubts can be raised as to the extent to which certain governments would be willing to submit to such a majority decision on this important issue, which potentially also strongly affects their domestic policies and arrangements. After all, apart from cost considerations, various political and constitutional reasons are also conceivable that might make it seem inexpedient for governments to take such a step at a given time. Instead of introducing direct elections against their will, governments would likely choose the option of terminating their participation in the body in this case. Even the attempt to install a uniform transitional procedure based on majority voting in the statutes of the UNPA or via a later decision might therefore prove difficult.

A two-phase model would be much easier to implement if the states agreed to include an opt-out clause in a majority decision to introduce direct elections. In this case, a large number of states would be able to make the transition together, while the rest would be able to retain indirect selection by parliaments.

---

[133] Art. 39(2) of the Charter of Fundamental Rights of the EU.

A flexible approach recommended

Our recommendation is a flexible approach at the beginning, leaving each state to choose when to move to direct elections. The assembly thus may initially be composed of national - and possibly regional – parliamentarians, but its statutes already in the first step should "allow the participating states to opt for direct elections of their delegates if they wish to do so".[134] Should states decide to allow for the possibility of the selection of delegates by parliaments from among the entire citizenship, this would have to be considered a further provisional solution pending the introduction of direct elections. However, despite the challenges mentioned above, we recommend that the objective of universal direct elections in all states be explicitly laid down in the statutes. In this case, a compromise could be to set no time frame for when this transition should happen.

Other modalities

Apart from the direct election of UNPA members, other election modalities can be identified, which states and relevant groups can choose to implement voluntarily, for example to achieve full gender equality or an adequate representation of ethnic groups in multi-ethnic states. As Joseph Schwartzberg rightly suggested, a global parliamentary assembly should be as inclusive as possible.[135]

It should also be pointed out that direct elections to the UNPA could be organized primarily in a digital form in the future. This would be convenient for the voters and could save considerable costs. This possibility, however, requires a procedure that can be applied in all countries and which in particular allows for a clear personal identification, a secure and verifiable counting of the votes as well as the highest possible protection against manipulation. These preconditions cannot currently be satisfied.

4.4. Key elements of electoral regulations

The prospect of a smooth transition from the selection of UNPA delegates by parliaments to direct popular elections emphasizes the importance of a set of rules that can structure the further development of the UNPA from the very beginning. Uncertainty about possible later changes should be avoided. An

---

[134] CUNPA, 2007b.
[135] Schwartzberg, 2013, p. 42f.

arbitrary variety of election modalities and development speeds is also undesirable. This would impair the coherence and transparency of the assembly.

The founding documents should contain comprehensive electoral regulations. Particularly with a view to the transition to direct elections, it is desirable to lay down important provisions right away, instead of leaving this to future negotiations which may turn out to be difficult. For example, it should be stipulated from the outset that a mandate as a member of the UNPA obtained through direct elections is incompatible with a simultaneous mandate in another parliament, a government office or a high-ranking position in civil service.

In the case of direct elections, it is essential to determine which uniform provisions must be applied and what can be regulated by national rules. Elections to the EP, for example, are governed both by European law, which is binding on all member states, and by national legislation, which may vary from country to country. The latter concerns, for example, details of the electoral system and the breakdown of constituencies.

Proportional representation

States could agree on a general system of proportional representation along the lines of the EP elections. Candidacies would thus only be permitted via party lists. The main arguments in favour of such an approach are the goals to be linked with a UNPA, namely the best possible representation of the different political currents of a country and the development of transnational cooperation among them. According to the concept presented here, there should only be one general procedure that is binding for all countries and allows for the best possible representation of all political forces represented in a parliament or among the population according to their respective strength. In the case of indirect elections by the parliament, a procedure would have to be established to ensure representation of the parliamentary opposition.

The timing of elections

It is a fundamental question whether direct elections can take place on the same day or within a certain short period of time in all UNPA member states where they have been introduced. The alternative is a continuously changing composition of delegates due to different election dates, as practiced for example in the PAP according to Article 5(3) of the Founding Protocol (alt-

hough these elections are not direct elections). In this case, it is up to the respective states to determine the timing of the elections, which means that delegates enter and leave the assembly on a continuous basis.

The great advantage of this procedure is the possibility to combine direct
elections to the UNPA with national parliamentary elections and thus to reduce their costs quite considerably. This would remove what is probably a
major practical obstacle to the introduction of direct elections in many countries. The price for this, however, is not only an asynchronicity of mandate
periods, but also a different length of the mandate of the members of parliament according to the national legislative periods. For example, one part of
the UNPA members would be mandated for four years, while another part
would serve for five years. Conversely, holding direct elections at a common
date globally would entail more effort, but would create more continuity and
attract a lot of public attention for the world elections. Initially, however, we
believe that combining elections at the national level at the discretion of member states is advisable for pragmatic reasons.

The approach of regulating the modalities of parliamentary and direct
elections in parallel from the outset would not only strengthen the democratic
authority of the assembly, but also benefit its capacity to evolve gradually.
States could move forward at any time without coming into conflict with
those less inclined to do so. And to the extent that the population could be
directly involved in elections to the UNPA in different countries, the pressure
on other societies to take this step as well would increase.

Gender balance

Another requirement is the establishment of parity in the representation of
genders. Some international institutions have already taken steps on this issue. For example, according to Article 4(2) of the PAP Statutes, at least one
member of the uniform five-member country delegations must be female. As
soon as the Malabo Protocol on PAP reform adopted in 2014 receives the
necessary number of ratifications, this number will be increased to two in accordance with Article 4(3), which means that the proportion of women will
then be at least 40%.

We recommend that a general minimum quota of about one third be made
binding for the first stage of a UNPA whereas individual states could set more
ambitious standards for themselves. In further steps, an approximate parity
between female and male members of parliament should be realized.

The concrete implementation of a minimum quota would be the responsibility of the parliamentary groups or political alliances formed for the election to the UNPA on the basis of the general election mode we recommend. These would have to be directly responsible for ensuring an appropriate proportion of men and women in the case of elections to the UNPA by national parliaments. In case of direct elections, this requirement would have to be taken into account when drawing up the election lists.

While the realization of such a quota at each election seems possible for states with a sufficiently large number of allocated UNPA seats, a long-term perspective and consideration of rotation procedures is necessary with respect to the numerous small states.

For instance, if only two seats are allocated to a state and if both the government and the opposition are represented in the assembly in the case of an indirect election by parliament, a practical problem arises: In case the government group chooses a male representative, for example, the representation of the opposition would automatically have to be female - and vice versa. Furthermore, it would then have to be regulated which side has the right of first choice in this matter.

This problem can be addressed by requiring the political groups to implement the regulation over several legislative periods. In the above example of a state with two seats, both the government and opposition groups would only be allowed to send a person of the same gender a maximum of two times in a row, independently of the other group. If, on the other hand, direct elections were held in this state, a minimum quota could be implemented in the party lists at each election and the population would be left to decide.

An independent electoral commission

The proper conduct of the elections to the UNPA should be prepared, observed and monitored by an independent election commission specifically established for this purpose, which should also be given the power to impose sanctions. Conceivable options would include the possibility of public reprimands or temporary restrictions on the parliamentary work of individual members or certain political groups, for example reducing speaking times or opportunities to participate in committees. In serious cases, certain delegates or delegations could be rejected by the commission or their voting rights could be suspended. For reasons of fairness, however, such measures may not be taken across the board against all delegates from certain countries, but only against specific individual members or political groups to which misdemeanours can be attributed in concrete terms.

5. The allocation of seats

A key issue to be negotiated in the run-up to the creation of a UNPA concerns the number of representatives that can be sent from each country. When evaluating possible models for the distribution of seats, an upper limit for the total number of delegates must be assumed as the practicality and efficiency of the assembly would be adversely affected if it was too large. We therefore recommend that the highest possible total number should not exceed 1,000 members. The models we examined range from about 700 to 800 delegates.

In order to achieve a mutually acceptable balance between the participating member states in the negotiations on the statutes, various possibilities for weighted representation provide solutions.[136] The application of such models represents an attempt to reflect the demographic weight of the individual countries as fairly as possible in the number of UNPA seats allocated to them, while at the same time avoiding the marginalization of smaller states or putting large states at too great a disadvantage. This is not possible without deviating from the guiding principle of electoral equality ("one person, one vote") applied in parliamentary elections in democratic states. This principle of equal weight of each vote is desirable in the long term as a standard for a future world democracy. With this in mind, a certain form of weighted seat distribution would not be a permanent solution *ad infinitum*. Moreover, any reflection of demographic conditions must leave room for change as they shift over time. In a broader view of the future, Joseph Schwartzberg pointed out that global representation of the world population can, from the outset, be presented as an evolutionary path. In the course of the expansion of the UNPA, this not only includes the transition from parliamentary elections to direct elections, but also the transition from a weighted distribution of seats to a model that fully complies with the principle of electoral equality.[137]

5.1. A uniform number of seats per country

The need to start with weighted representation, following the example of existing IPIs such as PACE or the EP, becomes clear with regard to the possible

---

[136] See in detail Bummel, 2010.
[137] Schwartzberg, 2012 and 2013.

pure representational forms. One of them is embodied by the composition of the UN General Assembly, where states are granted one vote and one seat in accordance with the principle of "sovereign equality". This means that China, the most populous UN member state with around 1.35 billion inhabitants, has the same weight as Nauru, the least populous state with roughly 9,000 inhabitants. Due to the large number of countries with a small population - of the 193 UN member states, 105 have less than ten million inhabitants, around 80 have less than five million, and around 40 have less than one million - there can be enormous distortions in votes within the General Assembly with regard to the population they purport to represent. Thus, the 128 members with the smallest population can theoretically provide the two-thirds majority required for important decisions, even though only about 8.4 percent of humanity lives in these states combined. Moreover, the 65 members with the smallest population are mathematically sufficiently strong to block a decision by a two-thirds majority, even though they represent less than one percent of the population of all member states.[138]

Given these disparities, it is not surprising that General Assembly resolutions are often adopted by consensus and in many cases enjoy little respect. Decisions with practical implications are implemented via a large number of other international forums. For a UNPA representing the people, a system of this kind that is based solely on the principle of sovereign equality of states is not appropriate, among other things because this contradicts the principles of electoral equality too strongly.

5.2. Direct proportionality

The other pure form is to project the domestically developed principle of electoral equality 1:1 onto the UNPA and to allocate the number of representatives directly proportional to the share of a country in the world population. In this case, 153 countries or almost 80 percent of the UN's member states would have three or less seats each in an assembly with 800 seats. About 70 states with less than four million inhabitants each would not qualify for any seat at all. At the other end of the scale, China and India would receive 159 and 138 seats respectively, making up a combined 37 percent of delegates. It is obvious that such a dominance of a few countries while excluding representation from more than a third of the world's states, is not appropriate and cannot be accepted whilst the nation state is such a dominant political entity.

---

[138]   See also Schwartzberg, 2013, p. 17.

An international survey conducted in 2007[139] suggests that this approach also receives little public support (see table 3). It included the question "How likely would you be to support a Global Parliament, where votes are based on country population sizes, and the global parliament is able to make binding policies?" There was majority support in only eight of the 15 countries covered. Although the reasons for the rejection were not asked, it can be speculated that the enormous differences in population size and the resulting distribution of seats were part of the assessment.[140]

In contrast, the establishment of a supranational organization that can make binding global decisions to combat global risks received majority support in all eight countries covered in another more recent representative survey (see table 4).[141] In this case, the question of the distribution of votes was not addressed.

5.3. Degressive proportionality

In their pure forms, the criteria of equality of states or equality of people lead either to the marginalization of small or large states. In order to balance the representation of political entities of very different size in a common institution, the principle of degressive, i.e. decreasing, proportionality can be applied. This means that populous states are generally allocated more seats than less populous states, but the latter are allocated more seats *per inhabitant* than the former. We recommend that this principle should be applied to the allocation of seats in a UNPA.[142] Within this framework, many different approaches, weightings, and formulas are possible.

At this point, it is worthwhile to first take a look at existing IPIs with weighted representation as practical examples.[143] The exact distribution is usually the result of intergovernmental negotiations in which different numbers of seats are agreed upon, particularly with regard to the size and political weight of the countries involved. However, the parameters applied are rarely systematically identified or determined by a uniform formula.

Accordingly, often no general formula for representation is part of the respective treaties and statutes. Instead, a concrete list with the number of agreed seats per country is often drawn up and renegotiated if necessary. This

---

[139] Synovate, 2007.
[140] See Bummel, 2010, p. 25-27.
[141] Global Challenges Foundation, 2018, p. 6.
[142] Following CUNPA, 2010, point 9.
[143] There are also examples at the national level, in particular the distribution of seats in the Rajya Sabha, the Indian upper house, in which the states and union territories are represented.

Table 3: Survey commissioned by BBC (2007) in order of the difference between positive and negative responses: "How likely would you be to support a Global Parliament, where votes are based on country population sizes, and the global parliament is able to make binding policies?"[144]

Country	Positive (%)	Negative (%)	Undecided (%)	Difference pos. & neg.
India	63.8	5.3	15.5	58.5
Dubai	58.0	18.4	12.4	39.6
Germany	48.9	29.5	15.0	19.4
Poland	46.3	27.4	18.5	18.9
South Korea	39.0	24.5	28.9	14.5
South Africa	46.7	36.2	9.9	10.5
Singapore	34.1	26.8	25.5	7.3
France	45.8	38.6	15.6	7.2
Russia	25.8	38.8	20.2	-13
Norway	26.2	41.1	19.6	-14.9
UK	30.8	45.9	23.4	-15.1
Italy	28.2	46.5	13.0	-18.3
Australia	27.2	51.5	15.0	-24.3
USA	23.9	51.2	24.9	-27.3
Denmark	14.8	52.9	16.5	-38.1

Table 4: Survey commissioned by Global Challenges Foundation (2017) in order of the share of "Yes" responses: "A supranational organization places global interests above that of nation-states. Do you think that a new supranational organization should be created to make enforceable global decisions to address global risks?"[145]

Country	Yes (%)	No (%)
India	84	13
China	78	15
South Africa	76	20
Brasil	69	28
UK	69	19
USA	67	23
Australia	65	19
Germany	62	29

---

[144] Synovate, 2007.
[145] Global Challenges Foundation, 2017.

approach appears to be practical in the current international environment because the corresponding IPIs - with the exception of the EP - have predominantly limited and subordinate supervisory and advisory tasks, so that the interests of the states are only marginally affected and having one seat more or less hardly matters.

The examples of PACE and the EP

One example is the Parliamentary Assembly of the Council of Europe (PACE). It is currently composed of 318 members elected from among the 47 national parliaments of the member states. The number of seats allocated to each country is specified in Article 26 of the Council of Europe Statute. This article is supplemented by a list of the number of seats allocated to each state, which has been adapted time and again, particularly in the light of the Council of Europe's expanding membership. However, neither the Statute nor the Rules of Procedure contain general rules governing the allocation of seats. According to the current version, the smallest members[146] receive two seats and the largest[147] 18 seats, while the remaining states vary in between depending on their population size. It is interesting to note that the parliamentary opposition of each country should be fairly taken into account, which implies a minimum number of two seats even for the smallest states.

In the EP, the distribution of seats also follows the principle of degressive proportionality. Under the rules of the Lisbon Treaty, each EU member state will initially receive at least six seats, regardless of its population size. Additional seats are allocated on the basis of population size, but no general formula is used. Roughly speaking, states with a population of between one and ten million are allocated one additional seat per 500,000 inhabitants, and states with a population of ten million or more are allocated one additional seat per million inhabitants. Germany, as the largest EU member with a population of roughly 82.7 million, has a maximum of 96 seats and Malta, as the smallest member with around 493,000 inhabitants, has six seats. One MEP from Germany thus represents around 861,000 inhabitants, while one MEP from Malta represents around 82,000.

---

[146]   Andorra, Liechtenstein, Monaco and San Marino.
[147]   Germany, Great Britain, France, Italy, Russia and Turkey.

The democratic legitimacy of weighted representation

The different weight of votes in the election of the EP was the subject of constitutional complaints in Germany. The criticism was that the system represents a violation of the principle of electoral equality as an expression of the general principle of equality contained in Article 3(1) of the German constitution. Two rulings of the German Federal Constitutional Court contain statements in this regard which are of general interest with regard to a UNPA.

In its decision on the Maastricht Treaty of 1993, the court noted, among other things, that in a community of states "democratic legitimacy cannot be established in the same form as within a state regulated homogenously and conclusively by a national constitution".[148]

Furthermore, in a ruling on the Lisbon Treaty of 2009, the court again addressed and elaborated on the question of the democratic legitimacy of the EU: "As the representative body of the peoples in a supranational community, and as such characterized by a limited desire for unity, [the EP] in its composition cannot and does not need to meet the requirements that arise at the national level from the equal political right to vote of all citizens".[149] Further the court explained: "The basic democratic rule of 'one person, one vote' applies only within a people, not in a supranational representative body, which - although now with particular emphasis on European citizenship - remains a representation of the peoples who are contractually bound together."[150]

According to this view, a graduated allocation of seats in a global parliamentary assembly cannot simply be disqualified as "undemocratic". However, the court has pointed out that inequality in the EP is only acceptable as long as the national parliament "retains its own tasks and powers of substantial political weight". The required degree of democratic legitimacy at EU level thus corresponds to the depth of supranational integration.

The question of a democratic deficit of a UNPA based on gradual representation therefore does not arise initially, since the UNPA in its first stage of development will most likely have much more limited powers than the EP today. According to the argumentation of the German Constitutional Court, it can be assumed that weighted representation is still justified even after a substantial development of a UNPA into a supranational global parliament.

---

[148] Bundesverfassungsgericht, 1993, recital 93.
[149] Bundesverfassungsgericht, 2009, recital 271.
[150] Ibid., recital 279.

Direct elections as a prerequisite for binding legislative powers

However, there is a connection between the expansion of powers and the strengthening of the democratic legitimacy of a UNPA as it evolves into a world parliament. Indeed, the introduction of direct elections was a decisive step towards strengthening the democratic legitimacy of the EP and an important condition for gradually giving it more powers. Accordingly, a general or predominant introduction of direct elections could be a democratic precondition for the UNPA to be given the competence to enact binding international law within defined limits and policy areas in collaboration with a chamber of states such as the UN General Assembly.[151] In such a system, national parliaments could also be more involved in global affairs.[152] The question of the gradual introduction of the principle of electoral equality would only then be on the agenda in connection with a further expansion of competences. This is also linked to a further strengthening of democracy at the national levels.

At least two seats per country

As long as the selection of representatives of the world population in a UNPA and a subsequent world parliament is based on nation-states and not on approximately equal global constituencies, which could in part comprise several states, the essential starting point for the allocation of seats according to the principle of degressive proportionality is to determine a minimum number of seats for each country regardless of its population size. The allocation of such a minimum number is in line with the principle of equality of states and prevents them from being marginalized or not considered at all in a parliamentary assembly. This minimum number can be achieved in different ways depending on the allocation model. Because a maximum upper limit on the total number of delegates is likely to be reached with about 1,000 delegates for practical reasons and the population differences between countries are so large, a minimum representation cannot be achieved simply by increasing the size of the assembly.

Since a central task of a UNPA is to provide seats and votes to representatives of the parliamentary opposition in addition to members of government parties, we recommend models that guarantee the allocation of a minimum number of two seats to each UN member state.

---

[151]   CUNPA, 2007b. See also p. 60f.
[152]   Cf. Bummel, 2018 and 2019.

In the case of a parliamentary appointment, the first seat should in principle be filled by the leading government group and the second by the leading parliamentary opposition in accordance with the number of seats in the respective parliament. In the case of direct elections, the first seat could be allocated to the list with the most votes and the second seat to the list with the second most votes.

If, however, a state is allocated more than the two minimum seats in total, a method of proportional representation procedure should be used for allocation to the respective political groups or electoral lists.[153] Where a political group or party receives a minimum seat under the above principles, that seat should be taken into account in the overall allocation in this case.[154]

There is room for interpretation as to what can be considered a fair balance in the allocation between countries. This question will have to be resolved in intergovernmental negotiations between the states involved. However, in order for citizens to be able to understand the allocation of seats and for it to be as transparent as possible, we propose that clear criteria and a generally applicable methodology be laid down in the statutes.

In the following, we present possible models for illustration and discussion.[155] Which states might not qualify for a UNPA at all, because they do not have a parliament and no real separation of powers, would need to be examined in each individual case.[156] For our models for the allocation of seats, however, we assume the universal participation of all 193 current UN member states. The total number of seats could still be increased if non-voting delegates are co-opted.

---

[153] For instance, the so-called "D'Hondt method" is a widely mathematical formula used to translate votes proportionally into whole seats. See EP, 2019b.

[154] A constructed example to illustrate this: In a parliament, Group A represents 51%, Group B 29% and Group C 20%. Group A provides the government, group B is the strongest opposition force. The country has four seats in a UNPA. According to the model of minimum representation, groups A and B each secure one seat. If the remaining two seats were to be allocated separately according to D'Hondt, each of them would receive another seat. However, the two minimum seats are taken into account. This means that group A gets two seats and groups B and C each get one seat.

[155] The underlying figures for population size and economic power of all countries are taken from the World Bank online database as of 2018, accessed 15 December 2019 (data.worldbank.org).

[156] See above, ch. 3.4., p. 61.

5.4. Models for the allocation of seats

Model A: Two seats and proportional allocation

In model A, a minimum number of 386 seats is initially allocated according to the principle of equality, two for each of the 193 UN members. The maximum total number of delegates in this model, as previously discussed, should not exceed about 800, so that in the second step about 414 additional seats are to be distributed among all countries. This will be done in direct proportion to their share of the world population, with the mathematical result of the formula rounded up or down to the nearest whole number. Due to rounding, this model yields a total of 795 seats, which are allocated among the countries in 16 increments.

   In this model, a number of 143 states, or around 75 percent of the total, are allocated two or three seats, 32 have between four and six seats, and 18 more than six. The larger countries nevertheless receive far fewer seats than in the directly proportional approach discussed above without a minimum number of seats. The allocation of seats for the three most populous countries would be as follows: China receives 78 seats for 9.8 percent of the total and one seat per 17.8 million Chinese inhabitants; India receives 76 seats for 9.5 percent of the total and one seat per 17.8 million inhabitants; and the USA receives 20 seats for 2.5 percent of the total and one seat for every 16.3 million inhabitants. The five countries with the largest share of seats allocated are China, India, USA, Indonesia, and Pakistan. Together, they are allocated roughly a quarter of all seats (205), but they account for almost half of the world population. On the other hand, the 105 smallest countries, each with less than ten million inhabitants and a total share of the world population of only 4.6 percent, are allocated a total of 216 seats, or more than a quarter of the total. In terms of balance, this is a desirable result.

Model B: Allocation by square root and two seats

Model B is based on a method proposed by Lionel Penrose in 1946. According to this method, the voting weight of each country in a world assembly should correspond to the square root of the number of eligible voters.[157] In the following, this approach is applied to UNPA seat allocation.

---

[157]   Penrose, 1946. For further details see Bummel, 2010a, p. 27 and Schwartzberg, 2013, p. 48ff. Schwartzberg rightly states that a root other than the square root could also be applied.

For this model, it is again assumed that all UN member states participate and that they are each allocated at least two seats. However, unlike the previous model, the number of seats allocated to a country is first determined using the square root of the population in millions, with the resulting number of seats rounded up or down to the nearest whole number. As an intermediate result, the resulting assembly has a total of 781 seats. Twenty countries with a population of less than 250,000 would have no seat at all and 32 countries with a population of less than 2.2 million and more than 250,000 would have only one seat. In a second step, these countries are therefore allocated the missing number of one or two additional seats in order to achieve a minimum representation of two seats. This would create a total of 72 additional seats without changing the actual allocation formula.

In this way, model B results in an assembly with a total of 853 seats and 17 increments. The rough breakdown of their distribution is as follows: 118 states, or around 61 percent of the total, have two or three seats; 42 states, roughly 22 percent of the total, have between four and six seats; and 33 countries are allocated more than six seats. The distribution of seats among the countries is less steep compared to model A. China and India both receive 37 seats or 4.7 percent each of the total number (37.6 and 36.5 million inhabitants per seat respectively) and the USA receives 18 seats for 2.3 percent (18.1 million inhabitants per seat). The five countries with the largest share of seats, which also include Indonesia and Pakistan, account for a total of 123 seats for 14.4 percent of the total. The 105 smallest countries have the same share of 27.2 percent as in model A.

Model C: Economic performance as a factor?

The square-root formula in model B significantly reduces the influence of population size, but population remains the only determinant of the allocation of the number of seats. In addition to population size, other metrics have been proposed as determinants. Economic performance is most commonly discussed as an additional factor.

With regard to the weighting of votes in the General Assembly[158] or the distribution of seats in a World Parliamentary Assembly[159], corresponding proposals follow the shareholder principle. According to this view, influential countries should be disproportionately represented in international bodies to ensure their continued interest in the regulation of common affairs. This is

---

[158]   See Schwartzberg, 2013, ch. 2.
[159]   Ibid., ch. 3.

intended to counter their feeling of marginalization by a large number of small states. In order to achieve this, each country's financial contribution to the UN budget can be used as a measure, which is roughly calculated on the basis of its share of the world's overall gross domestic product. Furthermore, the argument goes that countries that contribute the most to the financing of global affairs should have the greatest influence and thus be represented accordingly in the respective bodies.

The most important example of the consideration of economic factors in an international decision-making body is the IMF. Although this does not affect the seats per country, voting rights are weighted according to the financial contributions of the member states, which in turn are based on economic strength. The inclusion of financial contributions in an intergovernmental organization like the IMF, which focuses on intergovernmental loans and financial policy measures, may in principle be seen as a reasonable and appropriate measure, but even here the legitimacy of such an arrangement is subject to constant criticism.[160]

In the case of existing parliaments and IPIs, the factor of economic power does not play a role. Also with regard to a UNPA, there are good reasons against the inclusion of economic factors, both from democratic theory and practical considerations. As mentioned above, a softening of the principle of electoral equality in an international framework can be considered legitimate and appropriate, but it is very doubtful whether this is also true if it is based on factors other than population share. A parliamentary assembly should, as far as possible, ensure fair and equal representation of the people. This objective is compromised when dividing lines are drawn according to factors that increase inequality. In the case of economic power as a criterion, people from poorer countries would feel left out. The dominance of the developed countries would be reinforced.

Nevertheless, it must be recognized that the functioning and acceptance of intergovernmental decision-making structures can be significantly affected by the marginalization of major contributors. In our view, however, the allocation of seats in a parliamentary assembly that serves to represent the population should not be the means by which this problem is solved. The consideration of this and other factors should, if necessary, be realized in the General Assembly as a chamber of states, for example by requiring qualified majorities

---

[160]   Thus, for instance, a system of double majorities was proposed instead: Chowla, 2007.

for certain decisions.[161] This is all the more the case since a parliamentary assembly would initially have a largely advisory function, and budget-relevant and binding decisions could only be taken at much later stages in cooperation with a chamber of states.[162]

Three factors and two seats

Despite these reservations, for the sake of a comprehensive discussion, we would like to present a well-known formula by Joseph Schwartzberg for the first stage of a UNPA[163] based on an equal consideration of a country's share in the world population (P), world economic performance (C), and UN membership (M). The percentage share of seats W is thus calculated as $W = (P + C + M) / 3$, whereby the value of M is always 1/193 or 0.5181 percent (assuming that all UN member states participate).

In a second step, the respective share must be converted into whole numbers. Schwartzberg suggests that W be divided by the smallest available fraction, which according to our data is currently 0.1728 (for Nauru and Tuvalu), and then rounded. Based on our data for 2018, this results in an assembly with 569 seats. Another option is to take a certain desired number of seats (such as 700) as a starting point and then calculate the number per country according to the share W by means of a rule of three and then round it. For the purpose of this illustration, however, we will proceed based on the first approach. In this case, only one seat is allocated to 108 countries (in the case of the other option it would be 75). In Schwartzberg's view, representation by one seat is more than sufficient in these cases. For our own model, however, we maintain the principle of a minimum representation by two seats per country and therefore take a third step in which all states with one seat are allocated a further seat.

In model C we thus have an assembly with a total of 677 seats and 15 increments. In this scenario, 164 states or 85 percent of all countries are allocated two or three seats; 15 states have four to six seats; and 14 states have more than six seats. The five countries with the most seats in this composition are China (67 or 9.9 percent), the USA (56 or 8.3 percent), India (42 or 6.2 percent), Germany (12 or 1.4 percent), and Brazil (11 or 1.3 percent).

---

[161] In the Council of the EU, for example, at least 55 percent of the member states which together make up at least 65 percent of the total population must vote in the ordinary legislative procedure. Similarly, financial contributions, economic power or CO_2 emissions could also be taken into account, depending on the subject area.

[162] This is another argument for a two-chamber system, cf. ch. 2.2., p. 27f., and pp. 95, 113.

[163] Schwartzberg, 2013, p. 49ff.

5.5. Conclusions on the models

The allocation of seats in a UNPA will best be based on the principle of degressive proportionality in order to strike a balance between the number of representatives from large and small states. The goal of a graduated distribution of seats can be achieved through a variety of different approaches. In our view, the distribution should be based on a uniform mathematical formula, with an upper limit of 1,000 members at most, while guaranteeing a minimum number of two seats per country. The formula should furthermore be as simple and clear as possible to assure that citizens can understand the makeup of this body. With regard to a UNPA, the inclusion of factors other than population share in the allocation of seats to us seems to be inappropriate and fundamentally problematic.

Comparing models A and B, both of which may in principle be suitable, it is noteworthy that in both cases the smallest 105 countries with less than ten million inhabitants have a seat share of 27.2 percent (see table 5). The main difference is that the square-root approach leads to a flatter distribution and therefore seems to be more adequate for the goal of balancing. In model A, there are only 18 states with more than six seats, whereas there are almost twice as many in model B (33). The highest share of seats for a single country is 9.8 percent in model A and 4.3 percent in model B, less than half. In both cases, however, it can be argued that the weight of delegates from larger countries is higher in comparison to their voting weight in the UN General Assembly. In this body, the ten most populous states hold 5.2 percent of the votes, whereas they would receive 32.7 percent of delegates in model A and 21.9 percent in model B. At the same time, it is noticeable that the groups of states from ASEAN, the African Union, the EU, and Latin America and the Caribbean each have more seats in model B than in model A.

There are no major differences in the weight of seats falling to electoral democracies (see table 6). In model A, the figure is 53.6 percent and in model B 52.3 percent. However, in model B, countries that are classified as partially free receive 50 seats more than in model A. This suggests that model B might be better suited to supporting democratic forces in transition countries.

5.6. Participation of international parliamentary institutions

It is conceivable to complement a UNPA with members from regional parliaments and parliamentary assemblies such as the EP or PAP.[164]

---

[164] CUNPA, 2007b.

Table 5: Share of selected states and groups of states in world population, world GNP and in seats in a UNPA according to models A to C

States/group	No. of states	Population (%)	GNP (%)	No of. seats Model A	% of seats Model A	No of. seats Model B	% of seats Model B	No of. seats Model C	% of seats Model C
All	193	100	100	795	100	853	100	677	100
Pop. top 10	10	58.1	55.7	261	32.8	187	21.9	230	34.0
Pop. under 10 M.	105	4.5	7.3	216	27.2	232	27.2	211	31.2
Pop. bottom 128	128	8.4	10.0	285	35.8	311	36.5	261	38.6
China	1	18.4	16.0	78	9.8	37	4.3	67	9.9
India	1	17.9	3.2	76	9.6	37	4.3	42	6.2
USA	1	4.3	24.2	20	2.5	18	2.1	56	8.3
African Union	54	16.9	3.6	176	22.1	226	26.5	122	18.0
ASEAN	10	8.7	3.5	56	7.0	68	8.0	36	5.3
European Union	27	5.9	18.7	79	9.9	94	11.0	84	12.4
GRULAC	33	8.4	6.7	101	12.7	118	13.8	83	12.3

Table 6: Allocation of seats in a UNPA according to models A, B, and C in the categories assessed by Freedom House ("electoral democracy", "not electoral democracy" as well as "free", "partly free" and "not free")[165]

States/category	No. of states	Population (%)	GNP (%)	No of. seats Model A	% of seats Model A	No of. seats Model B	% of seats Model B	No of. seats Model C	% of seats Model C
All	193	100	100	795	100	853	100	677	100
Electoral democr.	113	49.4	71.7	426	53.6	446	52.3	410	60.6
Not elect. democ.	80	50.6	28.3	369	46.4	407	47.7	267	39.4
Free	84	38.7	67.2	325	40.9	324	38.0	336	49.6
Partly free	59	24.8	8.5	220	27.7	270	31.7	153	22.6
Free & partly fee	143	63.4	75.7	545	68.6	594	69.6	489	72.2
Not free	50	36.6	24.3	250	31.4	259	30.4	188	27.8

To implement this approach, the statutes of a UNPA may contain a provision allowing groups of countries to allocate a certain number of seats allocated to them to international parliamentary assemblies or parliaments.[166]

---

[165] Data of Freedom House, 2019, retrieved from freedomhouse.org. Figures for population size and GNP are taken from the World Bank online database as of 2018, accessed 15 December 2019 (data.worldbank.org).
[166] Cf. the calculation example in Bummel, 2010a, p. 39-41 for the EP.

However, not all countries in the world are currently involved in such assemblies. Moreover, the degree of development of these bodies varies greatly in the different regions of the world. An easier way to implement this would be to complement the UNPA with a limited number of members who would be sent by some of the major IPIs to represent them as a whole. These delegates could participate in the work of the assembly without voting rights and in committee meetings as permanent observers with speaking rights. This would enable good networking with other IPIs and strengthen the UNPA in its role as an umbrella for transnational parliamentary cooperation.

5.7. The question of weighted voting

It has also been argued in the literature that the seats in a UNPA could not only be allocated according to a sliding scale, but in addition could be endowed with different voting weights following certain rules.[167] The voting weight of a delegate could therefore be based on how many constituents are represented. In model A, for example, there are 17.8 million people per seat from China, and in model B as many as 37.6 million, whereas a seat from Tuvalu or Nauru represents only around 6,000 people each, which is almost 3,000 or even more than 6,200 times this weight.

In order to mitigate such glaring disparities in electoral equality, Joseph Schwartzberg proposed in a model for the second stage of a World Parliamentary Assembly that the seats be distributed according to the square root principle with an additional system of weighing their voting power.[168] In this scenario, the voting power of a seat could correspond to the square root of the original seat determinant, i.e. the fourth root of the population size in millions, with 1.0 as the minimum value. A seat from China would thus have a voting weight of 6.1, one from the USA would have a weight of 4.2, and the minimum weight per seat of 1.0 would apply to 38 states. The seats of the ten most populous countries would have a combined voting weight of 38.8 percent and those of the 100 smallest countries 12.3 percent. The seats from 171 states would each have a combined weight of less than one percent for each country. A seat from Tuvalu or Nauro would still have a weight 500 to 1,000 times greater than a seat from China. From the perspective of electoral equality, ultimately not much would be gained.

---

[167]   See Schwartzberg, 2013.
[168]   Schwartzberg, 2013, p. 51f.

Nonetheless, parliamentarians from smaller countries would be significantly devalued. There would be second-, third-, and even fourth-class delegates. Those members with a lower voting weight would be more easily ignored in deliberations and negotiations.

The development of a constructive debating culture as well as decision-making analogous to democratic national parliaments could hardly be expected to happen in such a context. It is difficult to imagine how the work in the committees should function on the basis of differing individual voting power. In the committees, individual delegates are not supposed to represent their country but transnational political groups and their perspectives. However, weighted voting would mean that the country of origin of each delegate would always play a decisive role. There is also no single modern parliamentary precedent to draw upon.

At this point in time, a UNPA is not meant to reflect the most precise measure of global electoral equality but a plural and diverse representation of the world's citizens and their interests. Moreover, the parliamentarians do not have the mandate to represent their country but above all the interests of humanity as a whole. It is difficult to reconcile this approach with a country-based weighting of votes. Finally, it has been correctly pointed out that the complexity of a system undermines its legitimacy.[169] This is another argument against the weighting of votes, because the more complicated the assembly becomes, the less citizens will understand it and the less it will be accepted.

All things considered, we advise against the weighting of votes in a UNPA. The requirement of qualified majorities based on certain parameters can be realized in later stages of the development of a world legislature through the chamber of states, if necessary.[170]

---

[169] Monbiot, 2004, p. 86.
[170] On this see also ch. 2.2., p. 27f., and pp. 91, 113.

6. Functions and financing

6.1. A wide range of possible powers and tasks

Initially it was assumed that a newly created UNPA would largely be limited to advisory powers in relation to the General Assembly and only in further incremental steps be "provided with genuine rights of information, participation and control vis-à-vis the UN and the organizations of the UN system".[171]

However, it has become clear that the establishment of a purely advisory parliamentary body constitutes a too limited approach for many who endorse a UNPA. In a 2005 resolution calling for the creation of a UNPA "within the UN system", the EP advocated that it should be equipped with "genuine rights of information, participation and control" in addition to the task of adopting "recommendations directed at the UN General Assembly".[172] In fact, even at its first stage of development as the parliamentary assembly of the European Coal and Steel Community (ECSC) founded in 1951, the EP itself already had both advisory functions and a monitoring role that even included the possibility of a vote of no confidence against the High Authority, the predecessor of the European Commission.

Moreover, in 2007 the PAP called for a UNPA with the right "to send fully participating parliamentary delegations or representatives to international governmental fora and negotiations".[173] More recently, the EP argued in 2018 that a UNPA should "contribute to the successful implementation of the UN Agenda 2030 and the SDGs".[174]

There is also considerable leeway with regard to the concrete scope of advisory powers. Thus, the work of a UNPA could be primarily limited to the participation in resolutions of the UN General Assembly. However, it is also conceivable to entrust it with advisory functions in relation to a larger number of bodies within and outside of the UN system. Furthermore, depending on the desired scope of this activity, a whole range of complementary functions may be established, such as the organization of monitoring and research

---

[171] CUNPA, 2007a; see also Heinrich, 2010, p. 6, who anticipated a "largely symbolic and advisory role".
[172] EP, 2005, para. 39.
[173] PAP, 2007.
[174] EP, 2018.

tasks as well as international conferences or forms of cooperation with national parliaments, various political institutions, civil society organizations, and the population itself.

Enabling a UNPA to perform a broader range of tasks from the outset would not only increase its political weight, but also its visibility in the public eye. It would therefore be more difficult to defame the assembly as a meaningless "talking shop" - an allegation that would possibly be made particularly by the very political forces that previously attempted to keep its powers and tasks as limited as possible.

Initially, the scope of the possible powers of a UNPA would in all likelihood be outlined and limited by international law and political reality. If the UNPA was established as an integral part of the UN system, the provisions of the UN Charter would apply. Thus, a UNPA would have no authority to intervene in the "internal affairs" of states, any more than the UN as a whole. Even if a global parliamentary assembly were to be established by a different means than Article 22 of the UN Charter, for example through an international treaty, it would likely be based on the principle of non-interference in internal affairs. However, even on this basis, a broad spectrum of tasks is possible, allowing a UNPA to become a significant hub in international politics. Given the political will to endow the institution with appropriate structural, human, and financial resources, the following rights and functions[175] are amongst those that could be transferred to the UNPA from the outset:

Advisory functions and global monitoring

- Conveying opinions and resolutions to the General Assembly, ECOSOC, the Secretary-General, the Security Council and other UN institutions.
- Readings on draft resolutions of the General Assembly with the right to propose amendments.
- The right to submit draft resolutions to the General Assembly for further negotiation and decision-making.
- Consultation by the General Assembly and other UN institutions.
- Involvement in treaty negotiations taking place under the umbrella of the UN regarding the creation or modification of international institutions.
- Participation in further multilateral treaty negotiations.
- Involvement in major international conferences on global issues.

---

[175] See Childers & Urquhart, 1994, p. 176-181, who considered the EP for the discussion of potential functions of a UNPA; see also Heinrich, 2010; Bummel, 2010, p. 36-38.

- The right to submit legal issues to the International Court of Justice (ICJ) in accordance with Art. 65 of its Statute.
- Identification and referral of cases to the International Criminal Court.
- Authority to alert the Security Council to dangerous situations.
- The establishment of a committee on petitions to enable the submission and processing of appeals from individuals.
- Conducting election observations.

Information, supervision, and participation rights

- Parliamentary oversight of the activities of the UN and its specialized agencies in conjunction with the internal control mechanisms of the world organization, particularly the Office of Internal Oversight Services.
- Right to ask questions, request information and cite vis-à-vis UN officials.
- Annual public reports on the work of the UN system with the possibility of holding hearings on specific issues.
- The ability to establish committees of inquiry regarding important global developments, such as serious human rights violations.
- The authority to investigate allegations of corruption or profligacy in co-operation with the UN Office of Internal Oversight Services.
- Extension of the above-mentioned functions to the institutions of the Bretton Woods system and the WTO following the conclusion of appropriate cooperation agreements.
- Participation in the adoption of budgets for the UN core organization and other organizations of the UN system.
- Co-decision in the election of the UN Secretary-General and other high ranking officials of the UN system and conducting public hearings of the candidates.

In procedural terms, the implementation of some of these tasks and powers would be carried out by the General Assembly as an intermediary. For example, the General Assembly could agree not to elect anyone for the office of UN Secretary-General who has not been previously approved by the UNPA. With regard to the right to submit legal issues to the ICJ, the General Assembly could commit to automatically present UNPA legal matters to the ICJ in its own name. In this way, the General Assembly could de facto grant the UNPA its own rights without the need for amendments to the Charter.

Regional parliaments have particularly emphasized the importance of the UNPA's potential to make the UN system more transparent, accountable, and effective and thereby enhance its legitimacy and public visibility. The parliament of the South American community of states Mercosur, for instance, recommended the creation of a UNPA in 2011 in order to "strengthen the effectiveness, transparency, representativeness, plurality and legitimacy of the institutions of the UN system".[176] In the same year, the EP supported the creation of a UNPA within the UN system to "increase the democratic nature, the democratic accountability and the transparency of global governance and to allow for greater public participation in the activities of the UN".[177]

The supervisory functions associated with these objectives would be understood in the sense of parliamentary oversight based on cooperation with existing UN control mechanisms, such as the Office of Internal Oversight Services. In this context, it is essential that delegates maintain an independent and strong position sustained by the "genuine rights of information, participation and control" the EP demanded for a UNPA in 2005.[178]

Boutros-Ghali suggested that the supervisory functions of a UNPA should also extend to the World Bank, the IMF, and the WTO[179]. This could initially be regulated under international law by cooperation agreements with the respective institutions and later on by amending their respective statutes. One or more specialized committees of the UNPA could be dedicated to this task.

The results of the work carried out by the delegates could become part of a regular reporting on the activities of the most important institutions of the international system, which the UNPA would regularly present.

The involvement of a UNPA in important personnel decisions and in shaping the budget within the UN - and possibly other institutions as well - would be a further step towards increasing the transparency of the UN system and involving the population in its governance.

Conceptual work and coordinating functions

The consultative, supervisory, and participatory powers of a UNPA would be closely related to substantive work, which can in principle cover a multitude of areas and assume a wide scope.[180] Conceivable areas are inter alia:

---

[176] Parlamento del Mercosur, 2011.

[177] EP, 2011, para. bf); see also PACE, 2006, which underlines the possibility to reduce the "democratic deficit of global governance" in this way; the EP, 2018, para. m), states "increasing the democratic accountability and transparency of global structural policy and governance" as tasks of the demanded UNPA. See also CUNPA 2009 and 2010.

[178] EP, 2005.

[179] Boutros-Ghali, 2007; later on also endorsed in CUNPA, 2009.

[180] Compare the substantive focal points of existing parliamentary assemblies such as PAP or PACE, which consist in key political domains as well.

- Monitoring and regular reporting on developments in key global domains, such as climate change, democracy, human rights, economy, environment, health, and governance.
- Organization of working groups with experts, expert hearings, and international specialist conferences.
- Communicating the programmes and goals of the UN in the public political debate of the member states and vice versa.
- Monitoring the implementation of UN programmes and international framework; agreements, in particular the Agenda 2030 for Sustainable Development and the Paris Agreement to combat climate change.
- Monitoring the effects of global financial and economic policies and how they relate to sustainable development, food supply, education, health, and poverty reduction.[181]
- Implementing programmes to strengthen the rule of law as well as democratic and sustainable social structures throughout the world.
- Promoting the exchange of information between IPIs and, where appropriate, coordinating their work as an umbrella organization for international parliamentary cooperation.
- Drafting proposals to tackle global challenges, such as sustainability.
- Drafting proposals to reform the UN and the international system as well as making recommendations for the development of international law.

6.2. Substantive work on global problems

This list illustrates a wide range of possible tasks a global parliamentary assembly may already assume in its initial stage of development. However, the political will of the participating states and the allocated budget would limit the scope of the assembly's work and thus compel it to focus on certain responsibilities. Over time, however, existing powers could be expanded and functions added by means of corresponding decisions by the member states. Even under the conditions of the first stage outlined here, which does not envisage the transfer of supranational rights, there is a vast potential for the development of a parliamentary assembly.[182]

---

[181] CUNPA, 2009.

[182] Considering the numerous possibilities regarding functions and development of a UNPA that present themselves based on the UN Charter alone, it is incomprehensible how Deplano, 2019, can arrive at the conclusion that a UNPA cannot be created "without tearing down fundamental provisions of the Charter" and that it is therefore also impossible to establish it "via the evolutionary steps suggested by its proponents" (p. 32).

This holds especially true regarding the substantive work in which the advisory functions of the assembly would be embedded. It could theoretically extend to virtually all globally relevant issues and thus "contribute to finding new solutions in situations where the policies of governments are no longer effective".[183]

If a UNPA is established as a subsidiary body of the UN General Assembly, a broad scope is guaranteed by the UN Charter, and in the case of implementation via an international agreement, it could be determined by the contracting states. In both cases, a parliamentary assembly can supplement, interlink, and harmonize the ongoing substantive work of UN institutions and other international bodies as well as render it transparent. Moreover, a UNPA can set its own priorities. In accordance with its mandate as a parliamentary assembly of humanity, these may be seen primarily in the areas of democracy promotion, human rights protection, global sustainability, and the reform of global governance structures. In committees established by the assembly, these and other issues can be dealt with on an ongoing basis.

A clear commitment to the essential values of human rights and democracy as well as to international cooperation based on the principles of justice and sustainability is to be regarded as crucial for the moral authority of a UNPA and the orientation of its work.

Such an overarching mandate can be formulated consistently with reference to the UN Charter and the UDHR. It would normatively bind the work of UNPA delegates and render attempts to abuse the forum for the propagation of undemocratic, discriminatory, and divisive ideas baseless. We recommend that the statutes of a UNPA include a wide remit for work based on the UN Charter and the UDHR, in addition to appropriate rights of information, participation, and control.

6.3. An institutionalized network of networks

An important element of the parliamentary debates would take place in the context of regular plenary sessions of the UNPA delegates. It would be expedient if these could be held at least twice a year in the form of public sessions lasting several weeks. It would make sense to schedule one session during the annual meeting of the UN General Assembly in New York, ideally using its plenary hall and other facilities. Further assemblies, committee meetings, and conferences could be held at appropriate venues around the globe. Their organization requires an increased effort but would provide an opportunity to

---

[183] This expectation was already associated with a UNPA in PACE, 2000, para. 13.

communicate the work of the UNPA to a wider audience in different regions of the world. It would also make it easier for a UNPA to promote an agenda of its own besides cooperation with the UN General Assembly.

Outside of regular plenary sessions, a large part of the ongoing work would take place in specialized committees and other bodies. As a rule, the meetings of the committees should also be public. Beyond embedding the UNPA in the UN system and interlinking it with other global institutions, an important task of the UNPA, the political groups and individual delegates would be close and continuous cooperation with national parliaments, the various IPIs, and civil society organizations. Furthermore, experts would have to be consulted regularly. The UNPA would work as "an institutionalized network of networks".[184]

Interlinking through committees

The specialized committees of the UNPA would provide starting points for the implementation of these requirements. They could meet regularly, but not exclusively, with the involvement of non-UNPA delegates who are experts in their respective field in other parliaments and belong to the corresponding committees there. The rules of procedure of the UNPA or of the committees could, for example, ensure that the respective parliamentary committees from the member states decide whether to send a representative to a session of the UNPA's corresponding committee. The UNPA's parliamentary groups should have the possibility to co-opt additional observers.[185]

Such a composition of the committees would ensure a continuous dovetailing with national parliaments, even if the UNPA delegates are partially or entirely elected directly in later stages of development. The committees would also be able to deal with international negotiation processes. A certain number of members of the relevant committees could be directly admitted as a UNPA delegation to the deliberations of the respective intergovernmental conferences. The recommendations of the committees would be relayed to the UNPA plenary for final consideration and adoption and then be communicated accordingly.

The establishment of additional relations to significant global institutions would not only facilitate a better exchange of information, but also help to coordinate functions at this level. In addition, granting representatives of political and civil society organizations observer status at plenary sessions and

---

[184] CUNPA, 2013.
[185] See also pp. 22, 59 and 103.

possibly working committees of the UNPA - and vice versa - could be agreed upon. As previously mentioned, it is perfectly feasible that the IPU continues to convey and coordinate the positions of national parliaments in the global system in cooperation with the UNPA.

6.4. The inclusion of world society

An important aspect of a UNPA is its connection to global civil society. Early on in the campaign it has been emphasized that the assembly should "provide for strong and efficient ways to include civil society, in particular NGOs, and local administrations" in its work.[186]

Various organizational options can be combined to this end. Besides the previously mentioned possibility of an observer status, it is also conceivable that the committees of the UNPA co-opt additional non-voting and advisory members for a limited period of time. These could be, for example, representatives of NGOs working in relevant fields. Furthermore, the committees could directly incorporate information, recommendations, and expertise from civil society into their deliberations through hearings. Moreover, other independent bodies could be affiliated. In this way, representatives of minorities and indigenous peoples as well as of cities and municipalities could also be involved.

The organization of regular expert meetings and other events on the work of the UNPA across the world would not only enhance public visibility of the assembly, but also broaden the debate on matters on its agenda and provide new input. Furthermore, it would strengthen the relationship between citizens and their representation at the global level and integrate additional social forces in efforts to tackle common global challenges.

In this context, we support research on the establishment of a world forum of civil society and its connection to a UNPA.[187] Such a connection may create a useful interface between global parliamentary work and world civic engagement - both of which would be geared towards taking up the basic needs and concrete concerns of the world's citizens and translating them into globally responsible policies.

---

[186] CUNPA, 2007b.
[187] On a world forum of civil society see also ch. 2.4, p. 34.

A UN World Citizens' Initiative

An initiative for global citizen participation advanced by DWB and a global alliance of NGOs is the UN World Citizens' Initiative (UNWCI) that aims to introduce a collective right of petition to the UN General Assembly and the UN Security Council. Among other things, the UNWCI is based on the European Citizens' Initiative enshrined in the Lisbon Treaty of the EU, which grants EU citizens the right to submit proposals to the EU Commission. If an initiative can gain the support of one million people within one year, the EU Commission must address the proposal. A UNWCI anchored in the UN could open up the world organization to direct citizen participation in a similar way and contribute to establishing a global political public sphere. The UNWCI and a UNPA can be created independently of each other, with a UNPA being able to provide additional avenues of citizen participation which should in particular include a committee on petitions to which individual citizens can turn under certain conditions.[188]

6.5. Media presence and digital participation

A UNPA would be the highest-level and broadest democratic representation of the global population, but it would also be the one most distant from the citizens. In order to mitigate this inevitable remoteness, the engagement of member states' politics, society and media would play an important role. This would initially vary greatly according to the political culture among member states, of course. However, once countries decide to hold direct elections for their UNPA delegates, efforts to raise sustained public awareness for the assembly's activities would become significantly stronger. In this context, people would be generally and directly called on to engage with the work of the UNPA and to participate in societal debates on global issues.

Modern means of communication facilitate citizens' general and direct access to their representatives at the global level. The increasing digital interconnectedness of global society makes it possible to make the ongoing work of the UNPA transparent all over the world and literally "bring it closer" to people. An obvious step would be to broadcast and document plenary and committee meetings of the assembly online. Another measure would be to provide information on global issues and the assembly's approaches to solutions on a continuous basis. The focus must undoubtedly be on inspiring the

---

[188] Website: www.worldcitizensinitiative.org. On implementation see Organ & Murphy, 2019.

interest of the entire population with an easily accessible and generally understandable programme.

We also advocate examining the extent to which new information technology tools could be used to add innovative elements of electronic democracy to the work of the assembly. Thus, assuming a stable and secure procedure is viable, consideration could be given to supplementing the regular sessions with regular virtual meetings, which would greatly benefit the continuity and dynamic of the collaboration between the delegates from all over the world (and also help to reduce carbon emissions). This virtual public sphere could also be extended in an appropriate way to working committees of the UNPA, joint bodies with other institutions and consultative forums with representatives from civil society. Furthermore, "innovative forms of civic participation in a UNPA" should be explored, such as the possible implementation of "models of electronic direct democracy or liquid democracy" to enable citizens to participate in deliberations or influence decision-making processes.[189]

Transnational e-democracy presupposes recognized, secure, and transparent technical solutions that allow for the broadest and most representative formation of opinions possible. On this basis, it would be conceivable to offer citizens a way to petition the UNPA online or to link its deliberations with online votes of interested individuals, for example. It should also be possible to coordinate political and social actions related to the substantive work of the assembly through corresponding online platforms.

Such digital approaches are to be embedded in the more comprehensive perspective of bringing people together across borders and to democratically involve them in global political decisions. To the extent that democratization of the global system can also be advanced by developing forms of transnational e-democracy, a UNPA would be able to play a key role in this context.

Even if the UNPA would initially not be located in a distinct building, it could present itself as a common house of humanity in the virtual space that is easily accessible by people from every country to take part in shaping the future together with their parliamentary representatives.

6.6. Funding requirements

The size of the budget of a UNPA depends on the nature and scope of the tasks assigned to it as well as on the chosen institutional design. Whereas a whole range of functions are relatively cost neutral, others require their own organizational and personnel structures. A budget that is too small would

---

[189] CUNPA, 2013.

limit the agreed scope of action and thus the assembly's public visibility and authority.

At a minimum, funds for a permanent secretariat to provide the administration and organization of parliamentary work are indispensable. In addition, there are expenses for the official translation of documents of the UNPA, which can be reduced provided that a limitation to the UN's current five official languages can be agreed upon. In any case, the working ability and independence of UNPA delegates must be financially guaranteed. At least travel, accommodation, and labour costs for the most important sessions have to be covered by the UNPA budget. In case of indirect elections from national or possibly regional parliaments, there are no UNPA-specific allowances but bonuses may be budgeted, especially to compensate for the largest discrepancies in the remuneration of the delegates.

The construction or acquisition of a new UNPA building or special meeting rooms does not appear to be necessary initially. However, suitable premises for the secretariat and the committees must be found and financed. If a state is willing to provide adequate premises, this may be an argument to establish the administrative headquarters at the respective location. It should be possible to convene plenary sessions and other meetings of the assembly at the administrative headquarters.

An additional cost item arises from plenary sessions, committee- and other meetings. If, as suggested, further meetings of UNPA delegates and public events they organize in member states should take place besides the annual session during the UN General Assembly in New York, an additional organizational effort accrues according to the number and scope of these activities. Finally, means must be available and budgeted for media outreach and publicity-related activities.

Existing interparliamentary organizations as a benchmark

The question of whether the members of the assembly are elected by the parliaments or directly by the citizens of member states is of great importance for the estimation of the costs. In the first case, the budgets of existing international parliamentary assemblies are a good benchmark.

The IPU, which has a nearly global reach as the organization of national parliaments, had a budget of about 17 million US-Dollar (around 15 million

Euro) in 2019.[190] Among other things, this budget enables it to fund two plenary sessions per year at different locations, various regional events, four permanent working committees, and the maintenance of a permanent office in Geneva with 40 members of staff.[191]

A second example is provided by the PAP with a budget of 16.4 million US-Dollar (around 14.5 million Euro) for 2020. At least two annual plenary meetings are scheduled, which can last up to one month. In addition, the PAP maintains nine permanent committees and one ad hoc committee on various social issues. The secretariat is run by 74 staff members.[192]

The budget of PACE is of a similar order with 17.4 million Euro (around 19.5 million US-Dollar) for 2019 (the ordinary budget of the Council of Europe for the same year being 244.7 million Euro or 275 million US-Dollar). The organization holds public plenary sessions in Strasbourg lasting several days four times a year to discuss the recommendations and resolutions prepared by the six standing specialised committees and three special committees. These committee meetings take place both during these sessions and throughout the year in one of the 47 member states. For the year 2019, the budget included 11.3 million Euro (or 12.7 million US-Dollar) in personnel costs for the approximately 90 staff members of the secretariat.[193]

Assuming that a UNPA is composed exclusively of members of national parliaments, has a comparable range of functions and a similar number of staff members, its budget would roughly correspond to that of the above-mentioned organizations. If the assembly was granted a certain upward leeway due to the broad dimension of its work and the higher number of members compared to regional IPIs, such as PACE or PAP, the minimum budget necessary for the UNPA can be roughly estimated at about 22.5 to 34 million US-Dollar (20 to 30 million Euro) per year.

This amount can be covered by incorporating it into the regular UN budget, provided that the UNPA is established according to Article 22 of the Charter. In the two-year budget of the world organization, which amounted to 5.39 billion US-Dollar (around 4.71 billion Euro) for 2018 and 2019, the UNPA budget would have had a share of about one percent. Part of the UNPA expenditures that do not belong to core activities could also be covered by voluntary contributions of UN member states.

---

[190] 16 million Swiss Franc with an exchange rate of 1 CHF converting to 0.94 EUR and 1 EUR converting to 1.12 USD as per 6 July 2020. Figures in this section are based on those rates.
[191] IPU, 2018.
[192] However, after budget cutbacks in 2019, the PAP called into question whether it is still capable of working at all with the funds provided, see New Vision, 2019.
[193] PACE, 2017, appendix I.

In order to ease the burden of the direct levy, voluntary contributions to the direct financing of the UNPA by non-governmental entities, such as individuals, corporations, and other legal entities, could also be facilitated, analogous to Article 116 of the ICC Statute. A prerequisite for such contributions is the definition of criteria ensuring in particular that the UNPA's political and operational independence is not compromised by such donations.

The budget in case of the introduction of direct elections

Whereas the budget volume of a UNPA can be considered modest if the delegates are elected from parliaments, considerably higher financial resources will be required if they are elected by parliaments from the population or if there are direct elections. After all, in these cases it is not national parliamentarians who assume UNPA-related tasks in addition to their existing national mandate. Instead, an autonomous global mandate is established for which delegates would have to be remunerated accordingly. Even if an entirely directly elected world parliament is only a long-term goal, estimating its rough costs is worthwhile.

Assuming that 800 delegates are paid according to the standing allowance of the Members of the European Parliament - 8,932.86 Euro (around 10,000.- US-Dollar) gross per month plus expenses of 4,563 Euros (around 5,100.- US-Dollar)[194], this would mean a total cost of around 129.5 million Euros (around 145 million US-Dollar) per year. With an extended staff, the total annual budget of the UNPA could then be in the range of about 225 million US-Dollar (or 200 million Euro). In addition, there are expenses for the elections themselves, which could be reduced significantly if the elections of the UNPA delegates were combined with national or other supranational elections.

The budget of a directly elected UNPA would be of similar order as such of intergovernmental organizations like the Council of Europe (279 million US-Dollar or 248 million Euro)[195], the OSCE (155 million US-Dollar or 137.8 million Euro)[196] or the ICC (168 million US-Dollar or 150 million Euro).[197] In contrast, the budget of the EP with about 7,000 staff members amounted in 2018 to roughly 1.95 billion Euro (or 2.2 billion US-Dollar), but only approximately 1.2 percent of the total EU budget.[198] A budget of this dimension would probably only be feasible for a UNPA by increasing the overall budget

[194]   As of July 2019 (www.europarl.europa.eu/news/de/faq/14/uberblick-uber-die-vergutungen).
[195]   The total budget for 2020 and 2021 is 496 million Euros (www.coe.int/de/web/about-us/budget).
[196]   For 2018 (www.osce.org/de/permanent-council/381499).
[197]   For 2020 (https://asp.icc-cpi.int/iccdocs/asp_docs/ASP18/ICC-ASP-18-10-ENG.pdf).
[198]   For 2018 (www.europarl.europa.eu/news/de/faq/26/wie-gross-ist-der-haushalt-des-parlaments).

of the UN accordingly - or of a world organization with supranational powers succeeding it. Nevertheless, its size is an indication that in the course of supranational integration, states must also attach a great significance to parliamentary legitimacy and consultation on common tasks. This is crucial to prevent the perception of a democratic deficit and a lasting loss of confidence in politics by the population.

If a UNPA starts out as an assembly of national and possibly regional parliamentarians, as recommended, the member states should still be free to decide when they introduce direct elections of the delegates assigned to them. The presumably slow initial growth in the proportion of directly elected parliamentarians would probably not be a major burden on the overall budget and would only become more pressing over time. Since the additional costs for directly elected UNPA members cannot simply be passed on to all member states, it would make sense to establish a separate budget aside from the actual budget of the UNPA, which would have to be funded by the states opting for direct elections and according to a fair allocation formula. This budget could be used in a uniform way to pay in particular the allowances of directly elected delegates and their personal staff.

The significantly higher cost of an assembly with an increasing share of directly elected members is coupled with a considerable increase in its efficiency, of course. In particular, it would pave the way for extensive substantive programmes and oversight functions at the global level to be carried out by parliamentarians and their staff, who would be able to devote their entire working time to the UNPA. Thereby, global representatives could, in cooperation with the manifold activities of the UN, contribute more efficiently to improving the lives of the world population in many ways and give it a strong voice in global affairs. An investment into more effective and democratic global governance should be considered worthwhile and economically sound. If successful, any potential savings in the long run will vastly outweigh the tremendous direct and indirect costs of the governance failures of today's system which may actually cause a breakdown of modern civilization.

7. Prospects for development

7.1. From a UNPA to a global parliament

The concept of a UNPA combines a realistic and achievable initial step with a comprehensive vision of global change. Following the example of existing IPIs, a UNPA can be established relatively easily at an affordable cost and immediately fulfil important functions in the UN system. However, its significance goes beyond that: As a representative and democratically legitimized political body of the world population, the assembly would be able to distinguish itself from the outset as a catalyst for transparent policies in the global public interest and the structural reforms necessary to achieve them. In collaboration with progressive forces in world society, it would be able to work in manifold ways to foster a further democratization and integration of the global system - and in doing so also strengthen its own standing.

Further development of the parliamentary assembly would be relatively easy to achieve up to a certain point. For a UNPA established under Article 22 of the UN Charter, the sessions of the UN General Assembly offer a good opportunity to regularly consult and decide by majority vote on additional powers and tasks of the body. If it is instead established by an international agreement, regular conferences of state parties would provide the framework for the extension of the assembly's responsibilities.[199]

A new political space

The establishment of a UNPA is coupled with the expectation that the assembly would support the work of the UN and multilateral cooperation in general as well as strengthen their legitimacy. This should be in the best interest of the UN and a large majority of its member states. A UNPA would create a new global political space that attracts public attention and support.

The assembly and its delegates would carry out their mandate to get involved in political discussions at the world level, to promote their own initiatives, and to represent transnational perspectives, in particular with the view to ensure the "well-being of future generations as well as the preservation of

---

[199] The thresholds for amendments must not be set too high, unlike for instance Art. 109 of the UN Charter (veto right of the P5) or Art. 121 of the ICC Statute (requirement of a 7/8 majority).

the natural foundations of life on Earth."[200] They can play an important role working together with other institutions and civil society movements to create political momentum and pressure for appropriate UN and government action. Among other things, this impetus could play an essential role to reinforce the fight against climate change and the goal of zero emissions.

One likely focus of the parliament's work would be to involve citizens and civil society organizations in the work of international institutions - which would transmit initiatives for reform to global governance systems. Even below the threshold of a UN Charter revision and supranational competences, the influence of a UNPA should not be underestimated.[201]

The collective promotion of necessary political change and the exercise of a supervisory function would increasingly strengthen the trust of many people in the parliament and in turn confer an ever more significant role to the body. Growing popular support in the world should convince governments to pursue a corresponding process of further organizational and legal development of the assembly.[202]

A particularly important step would be to extend the parliamentary advisory and supervisory functions of the UNPA beyond the UN to the IMF, the World Bank, and the WTO through appropriate cooperation agreements. These institutions not only exert enormous influence on the global financial system and world trade, but also on national economies. They have been criticized for a long time, among other things because of a lack of transparency, undemocratic decision-making processes, the undermining of human rights, social, and ecological standards as well as problematic repercussions, especially on economies in the global South. A UNPA could "monitor the interlinkage and impact of the system's financial and economic policies in other fields such as sustainable development, food supply, education, health or eradication of poverty" and "help to raise awareness of critical developments before they erupt."[203]

Moreover, the delegates would be able to work towards the creation of a just and sustainable world economic order in other respects. For example, the body could be entrusted with a role in the implementation of the Agenda 2030 adopted by the UN, as proposed by the EP.

---

[200] According to the call by CUNPA, 2007a.
[201] Cf. also ch. 6.
[202] On the expansion of competences and responsibilities see also Leinen & Bummel, 2018, p. 371ff.
[203] CUNPA, 2009.

An agreement on voluntary framework legislation is also conceivable. UNPA delegates could be mandated to draft regulations for certain transnational matters in cooperation with government representatives and other global institutions, which could then be translated into national law by the parliaments of the state parties.

The assembly could thus be the starting point for the emergence of a group of states that use the UNPA to achieve enhanced cooperation and increased democratic legitimation for political action. Its example and political activities could significantly contribute to progress in defending and strengthening democracy and the rule of law as well as the transformation of the UN.[204]

The introduction of direct elections

The introduction of direct elections plays a central role in the long-term development of the assembly. As the example of the EP shows, it would strengthen the position and self-confidence of the parliamentarians, since they could then rely on direct popular legitimation and focus entirely on their global mandate. Thereby, the capacity for a significantly expanded range of functions would be established.

As soon as direct elections are held in a majority of states, the body will presumably no longer be considered as a parliamentary assembly but as a world parliament. The willingness to introduce direct elections - and thus to grant the parliament a considerably larger budget as well - would confirm that the view has become prevalent in world society that global politics require direct democratic legitimation in order to be generally accepted and effective.

If states themselves can decide when to introduce direct elections for the members of parliament allocated to them, as we recommend, this development - unlike in the European example, for instance - would not be a leap, but a continuous process. Each country could set the right pace for itself. As progressive countries are moving forward, others could learn from their experience and it would probably generate political momentum in favour of direct elections.

However, the progressive introduction of direct elections would also highlight the contradiction inherent in a representative body of the people that only has mainly advisory powers in global decision-making processes. Sooner or later, it would be impossible to convey to the population that a considerable effort is being made to elect and mandate people from all parts of the

---

[204] Cf. also Soros, 1998, p. 287 and Leinen & Bummel, 2018, p. 94f.

world for global tasks if they can hardly decide anything. As a UNPA's democratic legitimacy increased, it would naturally assume a more active role in global governance which can and should include a key role in a global constitutional process that leads to a new world organization.

A new world organization

The transfer of legislative participation rights presupposes a legal framework for binding regulation of global issues. This is inconceivable without transforming the UN into a supranational world organization and the development of a global legal order.[205] A UN parliament would likely pursue this objective and mobilize the support of world society.

In concrete terms, this would entail an extensive amendment of the UN Charter as well as other intergovernmental treaties and effectively the creation of a new world organization based on a world constitution that integrates the current system of global intergovernmental institutions. In the view of DWB, it should be based on an equal world citizenship of all people and on the principles of federalism, subsidiarity, separation of powers, the rule of law, fundamental human rights, and the protection of minorities. The powers and tasks of this world organization would thus be limited to those that can be best accomplished at the global level, while other tasks would remain the responsibility of lower levels, such as regional organizations, individual states or below.[206] In such a framework, the world parliament, as the main organ of a world legislature, would ensure the democratic representation of the world population in global decision-making, and hold the executive to account.

We support the model of a global two-chamber system with a world parliament representing the people and another assembly representing the states. This institutional design and a world society that is increasingly organized democratically, equitably, and according to the rule of law would create the conditions for qualified majority decisions to enact global law in areas of global concern.[207] Finally, with regard to the world parliament, the gradual transition from a weighted representation based on countries to collective direct elections by the world population according to the principle of "one person - one vote" should take place in the long term.

---

[205] Cf. Leinen & Bummel, 2018, p. 379ff.; Leinen & Bummel, 2019; Bummel, 2014.
[206] See also Leinen & Bummel, 2019, p. 201.
[207] This includes the possibility of global taxation. Part of the revenues could be used to finance the operations of the new world organization and a directly elected world parliament in particular.

7.2. Parliamentarians as catalysts for reforms - the example of the EP

As soon as a UNPA gains more visibility and standing as a crucial global centre of political debate and programmatic work in the eyes of the world population and political decision-makers, the expansion of its powers and tasks
becomes likely: "As it established its credibility, as governments became more
comfortable with it, as its own institutional roots took hold and its informal
influence expanded, its formal powers would also grow."[208]

The EP represents an inspiring analogy for this prospect.[209] Similar to the
proposal for the first step of a UNPA, it started as a parliamentary assembly
established in 1952 under the European Coal and Steel Community (ECSC).
The competences of this Common Assembly, whose members were sent by
the national parliaments, were limited to advisory and supervisory functions.
However, in the course of European integration, the body was continuously
enhanced. In many respects, its structure and functioning now correspond to
those of national parliaments.

The history of the European integration process shows that delegates of
various political orientations have played a crucial role in both the overall institutional development of the European Community and in strengthening
their own participation rights from the very beginning.[210]

An important demand was the introduction of direct elections.[211] As early
as 1952, the Common Assembly presented a draft treaty for the creation of a
European Political Community on behalf of the member states. It envisaged
inter alia a directly elected parliament, a senate consisting of representatives
of the national parliaments, a supranational executive and a defence community. The initiative failed in 1954 due to France's opposition. Later on, the
1957 Treaty of Rome[212] stipulated at least the introduction of direct elections
of European delegates, which was not actually implemented for a long time.

Until the early 1970s, the powers of the assembly remained limited. Subsequently, important steps in European integration were combined with the
development of the EP, which in turn prompted further reform efforts by the
delegates. From 1971 onwards, the member states gradually responded to re-
quests from the parliamentarians to participate in the planning of the Community budget, and as of 1975, the annual budgets (with the exception of the

---

[208] Heinrich, 2010, p. 35.
[209] On the role of the EP in the development of the EU and its own strengthening see the publications of the
       European Parliament History Series on www.europarl.europa.eu/historicalarchives/en/publica-
       tions.html.
[210] In detail: Kaiser, 2018; Corbett, 2001.
[211] The initiatives of the ECSC and the EP are examined by Piodi, 2009.
[212] On the role of the assembly in the treaty negotiations see Piodi, 2007.

compulsory expenditure) had to be approved by the European parliamentary body. In 1976, the governments also gave in to the parliament's pressure to implement the agreed-upon direct elections, which were first held in 1979.[213]

In the early 1980s, an EP committee led by Altiero Spinelli devised a draft treaty for a new European Union shaped by a federalist approach, which received the support of an overwhelming majority of delegates across the spectrum of political parties in 1982.[214] Although the proposed constitution was not adopted by the governments, it revitalized the process of reform and democratization within the European Community, whereby the period of political paralysis at the time known as "Eurosclerosis" could be overcome.

Subsequently, many delegates pursued a strategy of small steps. This was reflected in corresponding recommendations and demands to the member states on the basis of parliamentary debates, among other things. Moreover, the body's organizational relations with the Commission, the Council, the national parliaments, and pro-European forces in politics and society were used extensively.[215] A major success of this work was the ability to emphasize the development of a politically sensitive crisis of legitimation, because more and more tasks were transferred to the European level without ensuring adequate representation and participation of the population.[216] This underpinned the political demands for a substantial extension of the functions exercised by the parliament. Since the agreement on the Single European Act in 1986, the EP has been involved in the general legislation. Its powers of participation have been steadily increased ever since. In addition, the parliament now exercises comprehensive supervisory functions in relation to EU institutions.

The work of the EP has gained appreciation among the population, including a desire of the majority to further strengthen its role.[217] The trust that the institution enjoys in comparison to others is noteworthy.[218]

Although the general conditions for the development of a UNPA and the UN system as a whole differ in many respects from those in the European

---

[213] Cf. Costa, 2016.
[214] EP, 1984; in detail: Bieber et al., 1985.
[215] Kaiser, 2018, p. 70-89.
[216] Ibid., p. 92.
[217] In a 2019 survey, an average of 54% of respondents supported a more important role for the EP in the future (10% wanted the role to remain the same and 21% a lesser role; 10% were undecided). In 25 member states, a majority was in favour of strengthening it, in 18 countries even an absolute majority. See Eurobarometer, 2019.
[218] In a 2018 survey, a majority of respondents did not only trust the EP more than all other EU institutions, but in 20 member states even more than their respective national parliaments or governments, Eurobarometer, 2019, p. 33

context, we have tried to demonstrate that similar aspirations of the parliamentarians regarding their work and reforms, comparable opportunities to exert political influence, and not least a mostly positive response by the world population can be expected. Similar to the initial parliamentary assembly within the EU, a UNPA should be able to act as a trailblazer and catalyst for an urgent international transformation, with which fundamental structural deficiencies in the organization and democratic legitimation of common global tasks can be addressed.

7.3. A call for participation

The first step towards a consultative UNPA may seem to be of little importance or urgency in view of the international power structure and pressing global problems. However, it represents a powerful political lever. For the global community, a UNPA opens up the opportunity for a "socio-political dynamic of empowerment"[219] that can enable the realization of a democratic world domestic policy.

However, this development is not a foregone conclusion. As an advisory body without inherent political power, a UNPA cannot evolve on its own. Without sustained interest and political commitment of the parliamentarians and global civil society, it would run the risk of degenerating into a shadow of its potential self - as one international instrument among many that attains little public attention, let alone further development. It would also be a mistake to see a UNPA in itself as a panacea for the world's political diseases and then turn away disappointedly when the medicine does not seem to work quickly.

Furthermore, it is not a given that the establishment of a UNPA automatically results from the political logic to which the numerous parliamentary bodies of other international institutions owe their existence. Notwithstanding the relatively simple feasibility of such an assembly and the substantial new functions it can perform within the UN, strong political resistance can be expected from certain circles as support grows. Greater civic participation, transparency, and accountability in the international system are by no means objectives that are attractive to all national bureaucracies. Moreover, the long-term development perspectives of a transnational parliament outlined here will seem too bold to some officials of the nationally and intergovernmentally organized world system, not to mention the advocates of nationalist, populist or authoritarian policies.

---

[219] Falk & Strauss, 2007, p. 70.

The realization of this project requires the active commitment of those people who wish for a different world order than the one we are living in today, a democratic world order that focuses on people and their home planet earth and is better suited to solve global problems. Without a strong international alliance of open-minded politicians, non-governmental organizations, and the citizens of many countries, a UNPA will not come into existence. Once established, the UNPA can in turn become the best ally of global forces of reform. It will open the international system to the concerns, but also to the creativity and engagement of many who are already committed to their fellow human beings or the global community as a whole.

This interaction could well decide whether the transformation to a humane, sustainable, and democratic world order succeeds before global crisis developments become uncontrollable and devastating. After all, it is part of the mode of operation of the current essentially anarchic, power-based, and fragmented world system to let initiatives for reforming world society, on the basis of the widely recognized fundamental values of civilization, come to nothing. Initiatives for change in the global framework have been stranded for decades, since the Hague Conferences before the First World War, in a political no man's land amidst the multitude of differently shaped foreign policies that are primarily oriented towards short-term national self-interest.

The successful establishment of a UNPA - which inevitably requires the approval of the majority of governments - would be a clear signal of change in itself. The new assembly would stand for the willingness to promote a humane and sustainable world order. It would express the will of the world's people to be jointly involved in shaping planetary policy. It would be a rejection of a global development that is characterized by massive violence, impoverishment, and oppression in large parts of the world, by the continuing threat of annihilation by weapons of mass destruction and the progressing devastation of the ecological foundations of life. It would also constitute the institutionalized antithesis to illiberal, egoistic, divisive, and short-term efforts in the world, which are indifferent to the well-being of others and of future generations.

From the outset, a UNPA would be much more than just a symbol and signpost. Through a new parliamentary forum at the centre of the UN, initiatives for necessary political change and structural reform could reach the global political decision-making process much more easily than they now do. Global parliamentarians would be explicitly mandated to give a voice to humanity and individuals in the intergovernmental political system.

Complex repercussions for national societies should be expected. The work of the UN parliament and its committees would provide guidance for the development of constructive foreign policy strategies. It would facilitate the organization of coordinated steps towards the further democratization and strengthening of the global governance architecture, simultaneously taken in many countries and contribute to the development of a corresponding collective "We"-identity of global citizenship. For the world population, a cosmopolitan political level - with a global parliament at its centre - would become expected normality over time.

The creation of a UNPA is only a first step, but an essential one. It paves the way for a new kind of world politics that allows us to shape our future collectively and democratically. This path must be taken now, before we lose control of our planet and our destiny. A UNPA is urgently needed and overdue. It must be demanded from the UN and the governments of its member states. We call upon all political and societal decision-makers, all organizations committed to the common good, and all citizens to join this cause.

Support Democracy Without Borders and the campaign for a UNPA:
www.democracywithoutborders.org
www.unpacampaign.org

Annex

Tables on the allocation of seats[220]

1. Possible allocation per political groups in selected countries

Possible number of seats in a UNPA allocated to political groups in the lower chambers of the national parliaments of the ten largest UN member states and the P5 in models A, B and C in order of population size and in case of indirect elections.

Country, election year, total numbers / Parties	No. of seats Nat. Parliament	% of seats Nat. Parliament	No. of seats Model A	No. of seats Model B	No. of seats Model C
China, 2018	2980		78	37	67
Communist Party of China (CPC)*	2175	73.0	78	37	67
Others	805	27.0	0	0	0
India, 2019	543		76	37	42
National Democratic Alliance (NDA/BJP+)	372	68.5	54	26	30
United Progressive Alliance (UPA/INC+)	112	20.6	16	8	9
Federal Front	47	8.7	6	3	3
Others	12	2.2	0	0	0
USA, 2018	435		20	18	56
Democrats (D)	235	54.0	11	10	30
Republicans (R)	199	45.7	9	8	26
Indonesia, 2019	575		17	16	10
Indonesian Dem. Party of Struggle (PDI-P)	128	22.3	4	4	3
Golkar Party	85	14.8	3	3	1
Great Indonesia Movement Party (Gerindra)	78	13.6	2	2	1
Nasdem Party	59	10.3	2	2	1
National Awakening Party (PKB)	58	10.1	2	2	1
Democratic Party (PD)	54	9.4	2	1	1

[220] We wish to thank Maher El Ghadban for assistance with putting together the first table and Liam Herbert for updating some of the data in the second table.

Country, election year, total numbers Parties	No. of seats Nat. Parliament	% of seats Nat. Parliament	No. of seats Model A	No. of seats Model B	No. of seats Model C
Prosperous Justice Party (PKS)	50	8.7	1	1	1
National Mandate Party (PAN)	44	7.7	1	1	1
United Development Party (PPP)	19	3.3	0	0	0
Pakistan, 2018	**342**		**14**	**15**	**7**
Pakistan Tehreek-e-Insaf (PTI)	149	43.6	8	8	4
Pakistan Muslim League (N). PML (N)	82	24.0	4	4	2
Pakistan Peoples Party (PPP)	54	15.8	2	3	1
Muttahida Majlis-e-Amal (MMA)	15	4.4	0	0	0
Others	42	12.3	0	0	0
Brazil, 2018	**513**		**13**	**14**	**11**
Partido dos Trabalhadores (PT)	56	10.9	2	2	2
Partido Social Liberal (PSL)	52	10.1	2	3	2
Progressistas (PP)	37	7.2	1	1	1
Partido Social Democrático (PSD)	34	6.6	1	1	1
Movimento Democrático Brasileiro (MDB)	34	6.6	1	1	1
Partido Liberal/Partido da República	33	6.4	1	1	1
Partido Socialista Brasileiro (PSB)	32	6.2	1	1	1
Republicanos/Partido Republicano Brasileiro	30	5.8	1	1	1
Partido da Social Democr. Brasileira (PSDB)	29	5.7	1	1	1
Democratas (DEM)	29	5.7	1	1	0
Partido Democrático Trabalhista (PDT)	28	5.5	1	1	0
Others	119	23.2	0	0	0
Nigeria, 2019	**360**		**13**	**14**	**7**
All Progressives Congress (APC)	217	60.3	9	9	5
People's Democratic Party (PDP)	115	31.9	4	5	2
All Progressives Grand Alliance	9	2.5	0	0	0
Others	19	5.3	0	0	0
Bangladesh, 2018	**300**		**11**	**13**	**6**
Bangladesh Awami League (AL)	258	86.0	10	12	5
Jatiya Party (Ershad)	22	7.3	1	1	1
Bangladesh Nationalist Party (BNP)	6	2.0	0	0	0
Others	14	4.7	0	0	0
Russian Federation, 2016	**450**		**10**	**12**	**8**
United Russia	343	76.2	8	10	7
Communist Party	42	9.3	1	1	1
Liberal Democratic Party	39	8.7	1	1	0
Just Russia	23	5.1	0	0	0

Country, election year, total numbers Parties	No. of seats Nat. Parliament	% of seats Nat. Parliament	No. of seats Model A	No. of seats Model B	No. of seats Model C
Others	3	0.7	0	0	0
Mexico, 2018	500		9	11	7
National Regeneration Movement (MORENA)	189	37.8	4	6	4
National Action Party (PAN)	83	16.6	2	2	1
Labor Party (PT)	61	12.2	1	1	1
Social Encounter Party (PES)	56	11.2	1	1	1
Institutional Revolutionary Party (PRI)	45	9.0	1	1	0
Citizens' Movement	27	5.4	0	0	0
Others	39	7.8	0	0	0
Japan, 2017	465		9	11	16
Liberal Democratic Party (LDP)	284	61.1	7	9	11
Constitutional Dem. Party of Japan (CDP)	55	11.8	1	1	2
Kibō no Tō (Party of Hope)	50	10.8	1	1	2
Komeitō	29	6.2	0	0	1
Others	47	10.1	0	0	0
Ethiopia, 2015	547		8	10	4
Prosperity Party (PB)	512	93.6	7	9	3
Tigray People's Liberation Front (TPLF)	24	4.4	1	1	1
Philippines. 2019	245		8	10	4
Phi. Dem. Party–People's Power (PDP-Laban)	82	33.5	4	5	2
Nacionalista	42	17.1	2	2	1
Nationalist People's Coalition (NPC)	36	14.7	1	2	1
National Unity Party (NUP)	25	10.2	1	1	0
Liberal Party	18	7.3	0	0	0
Others	42	17.1	0	0	0
Egypt, 2015	245		7	10	4
Free Egyptians Party	65	26.5	3	4	2
Nation's Future Party	53	21.6	2	4	1
New Wafd Party	36	14.7	2	2	1
Homeland Defenders Party	18	7.3	0	1	0
Republican People's Party	13	5.3	0	0	0
Others	60	24.5	0	0	0
Viet Nam, 2016	494		7	10	4
Communist Party*	473	95.7	7	10	4
Others	21	4.3	0	0	0
United Kingdom, 2019	650		6	8	9
Conservative	365	56.2	4	5	6

Country, election year, total numbers Parties	No. of seats Nat. Parliament	% of seats Nat. Parliament	No. of seats Model A	No. of seats Model B	No. of seats Model C
Labour	203	31.2	2	3	3
Scottish National Party (SNP)	48	7.4	0	0	0
Others	34	5.2	0	0	0
France, 2017	577		6	8	9
La République En Marche! (LREM)	308	53.4	5	6	7
The Republicans (LR)	112	19.4	1	2	2
Democratic Movement (MoDem)	42	7.3	0	0	0
Others	115	19.9	0	0	0

* no other independent party allowed

2. Possible allocation for all UN member states

Possible number of seats of a UNPA to be allocated per UN member state in models A, B and C in alphabetical order.

Country	Population share in %	No. of seats Model A	% of seats Model A	No. of seats Model B	% of seats Model B	No. of seats Model C	% of seats Model C
Afghanistan	0.49	4	0.5	6	0.7	2	0.2
Albania	0.04	2	0.3	2	0.2	2	0.2
Algeria	0.56	4	0.5	6	0.7	2	0.2
Andorra	0.00	2	0.3	2	0.2	2	0.2
Angola	0.41	4	0.5	6	0.7	2	0.2
Antigua and Barbuda	0.00	2	0.3	2	0.2	2	0.2
Argentina	0.59	4	0.5	7	0.8	3	0.4
Armenia	0.04	2	0.3	2	0.2	2	0.2
Australia	0.33	3	0.4	5	0.6	5	0.6
Austria	0.12	2	0.3	3	0.4	2	0.2
Azerbaijan	0.13	3	0.4	3	0.4	2	0.2
Bahamas	0.01	2	0.3	2	0.2	2	0.2
Bahrain	0.02	2	0.3	2	0.2	2	0.2
Bangladesh	2.14	11	1.4	13	1.5	6	0.7
Barbados	0.00	2	0.3	2	0.2	2	0.2
Belarus	0.13	3	0.4	3	0.4	2	0.2

Country	Population share in %	No. of seats Model A	% of seats Model A	No. of seats Model B	% of seats Model B	No. of seats Model C	% of seats Model C
Belgium	0.15	3	0.4	3	0.4	3	0.4
Belize	0.01	2	0.3	2	0.2	2	0.2
Benin	0.15	3	0.4	3	0.4	2	0.2
Bhutan	0.01	2	0.3	2	0.2	2	0.2
Bolivia	0.15	3	0.4	3	0.4	2	0.2
Bosnia and Herzegovina	0.04	2	0.3	2	0.2	2	0.2
Botswana	0.03	2	0.3	2	0.2	2	0.2
Brazil	2.77	13	1.6	14	1.6	11	1.3
Brunei Darussalam	0.01	2	0.3	2	0.2	2	0.2
Bulgaria	0.09	2	0.3	3	0.4	2	0.2
Burkina Faso	0.26	3	0.4	4	0.5	2	0.2
Burundi	0.15	3	0.4	3	0.4	2	0.2
Cabo Verde	0.01	2	0.3	2	0.2	2	0.2
Cambodia	0.22	3	0.4	4	0.5	2	0.2
Cameroon	0.33	3	0.4	5	0.6	2	0.2
Canada	0.49	4	0.5	6	0.7	6	0.7
Central African Republic	0.06	2	0.3	2	0.2	2	0.2
Chad	0.20	3	0.4	4	0.5	2	0.2
Chile	0.25	3	0.4	4	0.5	2	0.2
China	18.44	78	9.8	37	4.3	67	9.9
Colombia	0.66	5	0.6	7	0.8	3	0.4
Comoros	0.01	2	0.3	2	0.2	2	0.2
Congo (Brazzaville)	0.07	2	0.3	2	0.2	2	0.2
Congo (Kinshasa)	1.11	7	0.9	9	1.1	3	0.4
Costa Rica	0.07	2	0.3	2	0.2	2	0.2
Côte d'Ivoire	0.33	3	0.4	5	0.6	2	0.2
Croatia	0.05	2	0.3	2	0.2	2	0.2
Cuba	0.15	3	0.4	3	0.4	2	0.2
Cyprus	0.02	2	0.3	2	0.2	2	0.2
Czech Republic	0.14	3	0.4	3	0.4	2	0.2
Denmark	0.08	2	0.3	2	0.2	2	0.2
Djibouti	0.01	2	0.3	2	0.2	2	0.2
Dominica	0.00	2	0.3	2	0.2	2	0.2
Dominican Republic	0.14	3	0.4	3	0.4	2	0.2
Ecuador	0.23	3	0.4	4	0.5	2	0.2
Egypt	1.30	7	0.9	10	1.2	4	0.5
El Salvador	0.09	2	0.3	3	0.4	2	0.2
Equatorial Guinea	0.02	2	0.3	2	0.2	2	0.2

Country	Population share in %	No. of seats Model A	% of seats Model A	No. of seats Model B	% of seats Model B	No. of seats Model C	% of seats Model C
Eritrea	0.04	2	0.3	2	0.2	2	0.2
Estonia	0.02	2	0.3	2	0.2	2	0.2
Eswatini	0.02	2	0.3	2	0.2	2	0.2
Ethiopia	1.45	8	1.0	10	1.2	4	0.5
Fiji	0.01	2	0.3	2	0.2	2	0.2
Finland	0.07	2	0.3	2	0.2	2	0.2
France	0.89	6	0.8	8	0.9	9	1.1
Gabon	0.03	2	0.3	2	0.2	2	0.2
Gambia	0.03	2	0.3	2	0.2	2	0.2
Georgia	0.05	2	0.3	2	0.2	2	0.2
Germany	1.10	7	0.9	9	1.1	12	1.4
Ghana	0.39	4	0.5	5	0.6	2	0.2
Greece	0.14	3	0.4	3	0.4	2	0.2
Grenada	0.00	2	0.3	2	0.2	2	0.2
Guatemala	0.23	3	0.4	4	0.5	2	0.2
Guinea	0.16	3	0.4	4	0.5	2	0.2
Guinea-Bissau	0.02	2	0.3	2	0.2	2	0.2
Guyana	0.01	2	0.3	2	0.2	2	0.2
Haiti	0.15	3	0.4	3	0.4	2	0.2
Honduras	0.13	3	0.4	3	0.4	2	0.2
Hungary	0.13	3	0.4	3	0.4	2	0.2
Iceland	0.00	2	0.3	2	0.2	2	0.2
India	17.91	76	9.6	37	4.3	42	4.9
Indonesia	3.54	17	2.1	16	1.9	10	1.2
Iran	1.08	6	0.8	9	1.1	4	0.5
Iraq	0.51	4	0.5	6	0.7	2	0.2
Ireland	0.06	2	0.3	2	0.2	2	0.2
Israel	0.12	2	0.3	3	0.4	2	0.2
Italy	0.80	5	0.6	8	0.9	7	0.8
Jamaica	0.04	2	0.3	2	0.2	2	0.2
Japan	1.68	9	1.1	11	1.3	16	1.9
Jordan	0.13	3	0.4	3	0.4	2	0.2
Kazakhstan	0.24	3	0.4	4	0.5	2	0.2
Kenya	0.68	5	0.6	7	0.8	4	0.5
Kiribati	0.00	2	0.3	2	0.2	2	0.2
Korea (North)	0.34	3	0.4	5	0.6	2	0.2
Korea (South)	0.68	5	0.6	7	0.8	6	0.7
Kuwait	0.05	2	0.3	2	0.2	2	0.2

Country	Population share in %	No. of seats Model A	% of seats Model A	No. of seats Model B	% of seats Model B	No. of seats Model C	% of seats Model C
Kyrgyzstan	0.08	2	0.3	3	0.4	2	0.2
Lao	0.09	2	0.3	3	0.4	2	0.2
Latvia	0.03	2	0.3	2	0.2	2	0.2
Lebanon	0.09	2	0.3	3	0.4	2	0.2
Lesotho	0.03	2	0.3	2	0.2	2	0.2
Liberia	0.06	2	0.3	2	0.2	2	0.2
Libya	0.09	2	0.3	3	0.4	2	0.2
Liechtenstein	0.00	2	0.3	2	0.2	2	0.2
Lithuania	0.04	2	0.3	2	0.2	2	0.2
Luxembourg	0.01	2	0.3	2	0.2	2	0.2
Madagascar	0.35	3	0.4	5	0.6	2	0.2
Malawi	0.24	3	0.4	4	0.5	2	0.2
Malaysia	0.42	4	0.5	6	0.7	3	0.4
Maldives	0.01	2	0.3	2	0.2	2	0.2
Mali	0.25	3	0.4	4	0.5	2	0.2
Malta	0.01	2	0.3	2	0.2	2	0.2
Marshall Islands	0.00	2	0.3	2	0.2	2	0.2
Mauritania	0.06	2	0.3	2	0.2	2	0.2
Mauritius	0.02	2	0.3	2	0.2	2	0.2
Mexico	1.67	9	1.1	11	1.3	7	0.8
Micronesia	0.00	2	0.3	2	0.2	2	0.2
Moldova	0.05	2	0.3	2	0.2	2	0.2
Monaco	0.00	2	0.3	2	0.2	2	0.2
Mongolia	0.04	2	0.3	2	0.2	2	0.2
Montenegro	0.01	2	0.3	2	0.2	2	0.2
Morocco	0.48	4	0.5	6	0.7	2	0.2
Mozambique	0.39	4	0.5	5	0.6	2	0.2
Myanmar	0.71	5	0.6	7	0.8	3	0.4
Namibia	0.03	2	0.3	2	0.2	2	0.2
Nauru	0.00	2	0.3	2	0.2	2	0.2
Nepal	0.37	4	0.5	5	0.6	2	0.2
Netherlands	0.23	3	0.4	4	0.5	4	0.5
New Zealand	0.06	2	0.3	2	0.2	2	0.2
Nicaragua	0.09	2	0.3	3	0.4	2	0.2
Niger	0.30	3	0.4	5	0.6	2	0.2
Nigeria	2.59	13	1.6	14	1.6	7	0.8
North Macedonia	0.03	2	0.3	2	0.2	2	0.2
Norway	0.07	2	0.3	2	0.2	2	0.2

Country	Population share in %	No. of seats Model A	% of seats Model A	No. of seats Model B	% of seats Model B	No. of seats Model C	% of seats Model C
Oman	0.06	2	0.3	2	0.2	2	0.2
Pakistan	2.81	14	1.8	15	1.8	7	0.8
Palau	0.00	2	0.3	2	0.2	2	0.2
Panama	0.06	2	0.3	2	0.2	2	0.2
Papua New Guinea	0.11	2	0.3	3	0.4	2	0.2
Paraguay	0.09	2	0.3	3	0.4	2	0.2
Peru	0.42	4	0.5	6	0.7	2	0.2
Philippines	1.41	8	1.0	10	1.2	4	0.5
Poland	0.50	4	0.5	6	0.7	3	0.4
Portugal	0.14	3	0.4	3	0.4	2	0.2
Qatar	0.04	2	0.3	2	0.2	2	0.2
Romania	0.26	3	0.4	4	0.5	2	0.2
Russian Federation	1.91	10	1.3	12	1.4	8	0.9
Rwanda	0.16	3	0.4	4	0.5	2	0.2
Saint Kitts and Nevis	0.00	2	0.3	2	0.2	2	0.2
Saint Lucia	0.00	2	0.3	2	0.2	2	0.2
St Vincent & Grenadines	0.00	2	0.3	2	0.2	2	0.2
Samoa	0.00	2	0.3	2	0.2	2	0.2
San Marino	0.00	2	0.3	2	0.2	2	0.2
Sao Tome and Principe	0.00	2	0.3	2	0.2	2	0.2
Saudi Arabia	0.45	4	0.5	6	0.7	4	0.5
Senegal	0.21	3	0.4	4	0.5	2	0.2
Serbia	0.09	2	0.3	3	0.4	2	0.2
Seychelles	0.00	2	0.3	2	0.2	2	0.2
Sierra Leone	0.10	2	0.3	3	0.4	2	0.2
Singapore	0.07	2	0.3	2	0.2	2	0.2
Slovakia	0.07	2	0.3	2	0.2	2	0.2
Slovenia	0.03	2	0.3	2	0.2	2	0.2
Solomon Islands	0.01	2	0.3	2	0.2	2	0.2
Somalia	0.20	3	0.4	4	0.5	2	0.2
South Africa	0.77	5	0.6	8	0.9	3	0.4
South Sudan	0.15	3	0.4	3	0.4	2	0.2
Spain	0.62	5	0.6	7	0.8	5	0.6
Sri Lanka	0.29	3	0.4	5	0.6	2	0.2
Sudan	0.55	4	0.5	6	0.7	2	0.2
Suriname	0.01	2	0.3	2	0.2	2	0.2
Sweden	0.13	3	0.4	3	0.4	3	0.4
Switzerland	0.11	2	0.3	3	0.4	3	0.4

Country	Population share in %	No. of seats Model A	% of seats Model A	No. of seats Model B	% of seats Model B	No. of seats Model C	% of seats Model C
Syria	0.22	3	0.4	4	0.5	2	0.2
Tajikistan	0.12	2	0.3	3	0.4	2	0.2
Tanzania	0.75	5	0.6	8	0.9	3	0.4
Thailand	0.92	6	0.8	8	0.9	4	0.5
Timor-Leste	0.02	2	0.3	2	0.2	2	0.2
Togo	0.10	2	0.3	3	0.4	2	0.2
Tonga	0.00	2	0.3	2	0.2	2	0.2
Trinidad and Tobago	0.02	2	0.3	2	0.2	2	0.2
Tunisia	0.15	3	0.4	3	0.4	2	0.2
Turkey	1.09	7	0.9	9	1.1	5	0.6
Turkmenistan	0.08	2	0.3	2	0.2	2	0.2
Tuvalu	0.00	2	0.3	2	0.2	2	0.2
Uganda	0.57	4	0.5	7	0.8	2	0.2
Ukraine	0.59	4	0.5	7	0.8	2	0.2
United Arab Emirates	0.13	3	0.4	3	0.4	2	0.2
United Kingdom	0.88	6	0.8	8	0.9	9	1.1
United States of America	4.33	20	2.5	18	2.1	56	6.6
Uruguay	0.05	2	0.3	2	0.2	2	0.2
Uzbekistan	0.44	4	0.5	6	0.7	2	0.2
Vanuatu	0.00	2	0.3	2	0.2	2	0.2
Venezuela	0.38	4	0.5	5	0.6	3	0.4
Viet Nam	1.27	7	0.9	10	1.2	4	0.5
Yemen	0.38	4	0.5	5	0.6	2	0.2
Zambia	0.23	3	0.4	4	0.5	2	0.2
Zimbabwe	0.19	3	0.4	4	0.5	2	0.2

Documents

1. Campaign documents[221]

Appeal for the establishment of a Parliamentary Assembly at the UN, 2007

Humanity faces the task of ensuring the survival and well being of future generations as well as the preservation of the natural foundations of life on Earth. We are convinced that in order to cope with major challenges such as social disparity, proliferation of weapons of mass destruction, the threat of terrorism or the endangerment of global ecosystems, all human beings must engage in collaborative efforts.

To ensure international cooperation, secure the acceptance and to enhance the legitimacy of the United Nations and strengthen its capacity to act, people must be more effectively and directly included into the activities of the United Nations and its international organizations. They must be allowed to participate better in the UN's activities. We therefore recommend a gradual implementation of democratic participation and representation on the global level.

We conceive the establishment of a consultative Parliamentary Assembly at the United Nations as an indispensable step. Without making a change of the UN Charter necessary in the first step, a crucial link between the UN, the organizations of the UN system, the governments, national parliaments and civil society can be achieved through such an assembly.

Such an assembly would not simply be a new institution; as the voice of citizens, the assembly would be the manifestation and vehicle of a changed consciousness and understanding of international politics. The assembly could become a political catalyst for further development of the international system and of international law. It could also substantially contribute to the United Nation's capacity to realize its high objectives and to shape globalization positively.

A Parliamentary Assembly at the United Nations could initially be composed of national parliamentarians. Step by step, it should be provided with genuine rights of information, participation and control vis-à-vis the UN and

---

[221] In ascending chronological order. Also available at www.unpacampaign.org.

the organizations of the UN system. In a later stage, the assembly could be directly elected.

We appeal to the United Nations and the governments of its member states to establish a Parliamentary Assembly at the United Nations. We call for all organizations, decision-makers and citizens engaged with the international common interest to support this appeal.

Message from Dr. Boutros Boutros-Ghali, 2007

It is with great pleasure that I convey these greetings to the organizations and individuals who have joined forces to advocate for the establishment of a Parliamentary Assembly at the United Nations.

States and societies everywhere in the world increasingly confront forces far beyond the control of any one state or even group of states. Some of these forces are irresistible, such as the globalization of economic activity and communications. In the process, problems which can only be solved effectively at the global level, are multiplying and requirements of political governance are extending beyond state borders accordingly. Increasing decisionmaking at the global level is inevitable. In this process, however, democracy within the state will diminish in importance if the process of democratization does not move forward at the international level.

Therefore, we need to promote the democratization of globalization, before globalization destroys the foundations of national and international democracy.

The establishment of a Parliamentary Assembly at the United Nations has become an indispensable step to achieve democratic control of globalization. Complementary to international democracy among states, which no less has to be developed, it would foster global democracy beyond states, giving the citizens a genuine voice in world affairs.

As the Campaign's appeal rightly implies, a United Nations Parliamentary Assembly could also become a catalyst for a comprehensive reform of the international system. In particular, I would like to point out, it should become a force to provide democratic oversight over the World Bank, the IMF and the WTO.

We cannot just dream, or wait for someone else to bring our dream about. We must act now. In this sense, I strongly encourage you in your struggle for a United Nations Parliamentary Assembly. Once established, this new body will be a decisive contribution to strengthen democracy at all levels.

Conclusions regarding policies of the Campaign for a UNPA, 2007

At its meeting on 19-20 November 2007 in the "Palais des Nations" in Geneva, the Campaign for the Establishment of a United Nations Parliamentary Assembly (UNPA) has reiterated the policies laid down in the "Appeal for the Establishment for a Parliamentary Assembly at the United Nations" and notes in particular that:

- the Campaign pursues a politically pragmatic and gradual approach to achieve the eventual long-term goal of a world parliament;
- in a first step the Campaign advocates the establishment of a UNPA by means which do not require a change of the UN Charter;
- the Campaign's appeal states that a consultative UNPA initially could be composed of national parliamentarians and that this statement does not exclude the option to advocate the participation of other entities. For example, the Campaign also advocates the participation of regional parliamentary assemblies in a UNPA, such as the European Parliament and the Pan-African Parliament, and consideration may be given for the inclusion of local authorities in the consultative UNPA ;
- the aforementioned statement also does not exclude to advocate a flexible approach to the mode of elections. The Campaign supports the approach that already in the first step the UNPA's Statutes should allow the participating states to opt for direct elections of their delegates if they wish to do so;
- the Campaign advocates a UNPA which is inclusive and open to all UN member states. However, direct elections of the UNPA's delegates are regarded as a precondition for vesting the body with legislative rights.
- the Campaign policy clearly embraces the demand that a UNPA has to provide for strong and efficient ways to include civil society, in particular NGOs, and local administrations into its work;
- the Campaign's policy pursues the goal that the UNPA, once established, would advocate and facilitate a reform of the present system of international institutions and global governance;
- the Campaign understands that whereas the appeal refers to "the UN and the organizations of the UN system," that this could be interpreted to include the Bretton Woods Institutions.

The establishment of a UNPA and the Inter-Parliamentary Union, 2008

At its meeting on 4-5 November 2008 in the European Parliament in Brussels, the Campaign for the Establishment of a United Nations Parliamentary Assembly (UNPA) deliberated on the relation between the proposed UNPA and the Inter-Parliamentary Union (IPU) and the possible roles and functions of the two parliamentary bodies.

The Campaign concluded that the proposed UNPA and the IPU would be complementary institutions. A UNPA would not replace or duplicate the IPU's functions. Quite the contrary, a UNPA would provide a response to the democratic deficit in global governance which the IPU in its current structure is unable to offer.

The Campaign noted in particular:

(1) The IPU is an association of national parliaments. One of its activities is to provide for a "parliamentary dimension to international cooperation". The IPU's goal in this context is to strengthen the ability of national parliaments to exercise their oversight functions at the national level in matters of international nature. The Campaign underlines the importance of this dimension.

(2) The purpose of a UNPA is to exercise parliamentary functions directly at the international level in its own right. One of the goals is to make the UN executives and its institutions accountable to a global parliamentary body. The IPU has no such capacity and currently also does not aspire to develop such an oversight function.

(3) The IPU's purpose is to be a facilitator for the work of national parliaments. In contrast, a UNPA would be composed of individual parliamentarians who would be called upon to take a global view.

(4) The precedent of the Pan-African Parliament and the African Parliamentary Union shows that the UNPA and the IPU need not be mutually exclusive.

(5) In the long run, a UNPA could be composed of directly elected members. The precedent of the European Parliament and the Conference of Community and European Affairs Committees of Parliaments of the European Union shows that a largely directly elected UNPA and the IPU would be complementary and indeed both necessary.

(6) The Campaign supports the work of the IPU and appreciates any and all active contributions from the IPU and IPU members in the efforts for the establishment of a UNPA.

Call for global democratic oversight of international financial and economic institutions, 2009

Triggered by the global financial crisis, the world community faces a huge social and economic disruption. The achievement of the Millennium Development goals is seriously threatened. The poorest in the world are those most affected. Potentially grave repercussions on political stability and democracy are to be feared. The situation requires rapid and effective global responses. An appropriate institutional setting has to be set up to regulate and re-orient the financial system.

Multilateral institutions such as the World Bank Group, the International Monetary Fund and the World Trade Organization have created global policy with enormous impact on international trade, finances and national economies. At this critical juncture it must be ensured that any renewed system of international monetary, financial and economic institutions will be sufficiently mandated, more credible, legitimate, transparent, accountable, representative, responsive and more democratic. The setup of the reformed system has to guarantee that the world's citizens, those affected by its policies and decision-making, are able to have their voices heard in the formulation, implementation and evaluation of these policies. This task should be supported by the creation of a global body of elected representatives.

The establishment of a United Nations Parliamentary Assembly should be an important part of the renewed system of international financial and economic governance. Initially, the assembly could have a largely consultative function. In the long run, it could exercise genuine global oversight over the system's institutions. Such an assembly could

- monitor the interlinkage and impact of the system's financial and economic policies in other fields such as sustainable development, food supply, education, health or eradication of poverty;
- help to raise awareness of critical developments before they erupt;
- function as a watchdog ensuring that reforms and regulations are implemented effectively;
- gather feedback from the grassroots level and civil society, with special attention to the weak, poor and underprivileged;
- have a say in the election of the Executive Directors of the system's institutions;
- contribute to finding solutions for the pressing global problems.

We call on the United Nations and the governments of its member states to support the establishment of a United Nations Parliamentary Assembly in their deliberations on the reform of international monetary, financial and economic institutions. We urge the Commission of Experts on Reforms of the International Monetary and Financial System set up by the President of the UN General Assembly to consider the proposal and to express its support. We call for all organizations, decision-makers and citizens engaged with the global common interest to support this call.

Declaration of Buenos Aires, 2010

1. We, the participants in the Campaign for the Establishment of a United Nations Parliamentary Assembly, reiterate our joint appeal to the United Nations and the governments of its member states to start a preparatory process towards an intergovernmental conference for the purpose of establishing a Parliamentary Assembly at the United Nations.

2. Sixty-five years after the establishment of the United Nations, in the name of "We, the Peoples", the world's most universal political organization still is not equipped with a formal body that enables elected representatives of the world's citizens to participate in its deliberations and decision-making.

3. At the 2005 World Summit of the United Nations, the heads of states and governments reaffirmed that "Democracy is a universal value based on the freely expressed will of people to determine their own political, economic, social and cultural systems and their full participation in all aspects of their lives." However, in today's interdependent world, no society is able to determine its own fate independently and without the explicit participation and input of the people expressed through their elected representatives.

4. Those who are to be affected by a decision should have a chance to take part in it. As important decisions taken at the global level today affect all human beings, we recognize the need to democratize global governance. Therefore we confirm our determination that democratic participation and representation of the world's citizens is gradually implemented in the United Nations and, as appropriate, in its funds, programmes and agencies as well as other intergovernmental organizations.

5. In today's multipolar world, enhancing the institutional foundations of governance is more important than ever. In particular, there is an urgent need to bring about a more coherent framework of multilateral organizations, agencies, programmes, funds, and treaty bodies and to make these organizations more accountable to the world's citizens.

6. The United Nations system is and should continue to be the essential core institution for international cooperation and a more viable framework for effective international governance. A UN Parliamentary Assembly will be

a critical component, and a catalyst for further institutional evolution. We expect that once established, a UN Parliamentary Assembly, would advocate and facilitate more comprehensive reform of the present system of international institutions and global governance.

7. Global challenges such as climate change mitigation, nuclear non-proliferation, and financial stabilization, transcend national boundaries and can only be dealt with by more effective transnational governance structures. A UN Parliamentary Assembly would be a response to these challenges as it would be able to make international governance structures more democratic, more inclusive and would balance the relationship between small and large countries.

8. We reiterate our view that a UN Parliamentary Assembly can and should evolve gradually. In the first step, changing the UN's Charter would be unnecessary. Two options are available: A UN Parliamentary Assembly could be set up by a vote of the UN General Assembly under Article 22 of the UN Charter. Alternatively, it could be created on the basis of a new intergovernmental treaty. In the longer term, the assembly could be transformed into a directly elected legislative world parliament as a result of a UN Charter review according to Article 109 of the UN Charter.

9. Having considered different models for representation in such an assembly, we believe that the principle of degressive proportionality could be taken as a possible basis for the distribution of seats.

10. The need to democratize global governance is one of the greatest political challenges of our times. It calls on individual world citizens, and especially parliamentarians, governments, the international donor community, and civil society to make a commitment to democratic global change. Thereby, we believe, the UN and other global intergovernmental institutions would become more effective and deliver better results for people worldwide.

11. We now call on all governments that espouse democratic principles at home, and which proclaim their virtues abroad, to advocate and support the application of the same principles of democracy, accountability and transparency in international institutions and decision-making processes.

Declaration of Brussels: Toward a democratic and equitable international order, 2013

Recalling and affirming
- the "Appeal for the Establishment of a Parliamentary Assembly at the United Nations" of April 2007,

- the "Conclusions regarding policies of the Campaign for a UN Parliamentary Assembly" of November 2007,
- the "Statement on the establishment of a United Nations Parliamentary Assembly and the Inter-Parliamentary Union" of November 2008,
- the "Call for global democratic oversight of international financial and economic institutions" of April 2009, and
- the "Declaration of Buenos Aires" of October 2010,

1. We, the participants in the Campaign for the Establishment of a United Nations Parliamentary Assembly (UNPA), reiterate our joint appeal to the United Nations and its member states to advance the necessary processes for the establishment of a Parliamentary Assembly at the United Nations.

2. We express our concern that in the intergovernmental realm no adequate measures have been taken to address the democratic deficit of global governance in general and of the United Nations in particular.

3. We reiterate our view that a UNPA is a vital component to strengthen democratic participation in and the democratic legitimacy of the United Nations as well as other intergovernmental organizations such as the World Bank Group, the International Monetary Fund, and the World Trade Organization.

4. A UNPA would enable citizen representatives, i.e. elected parliamentarians, to be directly involved in global political deliberations, agenda-setting, and decision-making, in a formalized and institutionalized manner.

5. Global problems require global solutions. The daily lives of the world's citizens are increasingly shaped by economic, social and political forces that transcend national boundaries and demonstrate a growing need for more inclusive, effective and transparent global governance.

6. The universality of human rights and the necessity of a democratic basis for legitimate governance are widely acknowledged. Yet, far too many people are denied their human rights and democratic participation. We are convinced that a UNPA as a global democratic body of elected representatives would strengthen the practice of democratic governance and fulfillment of human rights regionally, nationally and locally. Conversely, we believe that excluding democratic principles and participation from global governance undermines democracy at the regional, national, and local levels.

7. We emphasize our conviction that a UNPA needs to be inclusive and open for participation of parliamentarians of all UN member states and observer states. We acknowledge that ensuring the democratic character of a UNPA presents challenges. We are convinced that these challenges can be overcome, and that with political will a parliamentary assembly for the United

Nations can be constructed in a manner that is both representative and legitimate.

8. We welcome the decision of the UN's Human Rights Council to mandate an Independent Expert on the Promotion of a Democratic and Equitable International Order, and encourage the Independent Expert to keep considering the question of a UNPA and in particular to examine possible processes towards its creation.

9. We welcome the recent and ongoing broad-based consultations among a wide range of governmental and nongovernmental stakeholders, to develop a global consensus on the Post-2015 Development Agenda. We feel encouraged that these consultations have emphasized (1) the importance of a "rights-based" approach to sustainable development; and (2) the necessity of a comprehensive, global approach, to address poverty and inequality in all countries.

10. The UN High Level Panel of Eminent Persons on the Post-2015 Development Agenda recently noted that achieving the post-2015 vision will require "reshaped and revitalized global governance partnerships" to ensure that "the United Nations, multilateral systems, and all development actors effectively support the post-2015 development agenda." Indeed, we observe that sustaining a multi-stakeholder consensus for shared global goals is one of the key functions that a UNPA would be expected to provide.

11. To maintain political support, to reinforce accountability and to bring global governance in the pursuit of post-2015 development goals closer to those directly affected, we encourage the creation of a UNPA when the international community adopts its Post-2015 Development Agenda.

12. A UNPA is a global parliamentary body that includes distinctive innovative features that go beyond the characteristics of existing national and regional assemblies and parliaments. Acting as an institutionalized "network of networks", a UNPA could allow representatives of existing parliamentary networks and institutions to formally participate in its work, thus providing them with more leverage and influence. Consideration should be given to the possibility of involving local authorities and representatives of indigenous peoples and nations in the activities of a UNPA.

13. We affirm that a UNPA can and should evolve gradually. Eventually members of a UNPA should be directly elected. From the UNPA's inception its statutes should allow participating states to opt for direct elections of their delegates if they wish to do so.

14. With a view to exploring innovative forms of civic participation in a UNPA, implementing models of electronic direct or "liquid" democracy that

allow citizens to participate in deliberations or to influence decision-making processes could be considered.

15. We congratulate the European Parliament on its pioneering role in promoting the establishment of a UNPA, dating back to resolution A3-0331/93 adopted in 1994, and most recently expressed in resolution P7_TA 0255 of 2011, which called on the EU Council to introduce the establishment of a UNPA into the proceedings of the UN General Assembly.

16. We call on the European Parliament and its members as well as on all other parliaments and their members to reinforce their commitment to more democratic global governance through continued support for a United Nations Parliamentary Assembly.

Call to Action on the Creation of a UN Parliamentary Assembly, 2018

The United Nations, the multilateral order and democracy are under attack. Business as usual and lofty rhetoric are not sufficient to counter this threat. Despite many warnings and recommendations, not much has been done to prepare the United Nations for this challenge. The time for complacency and complaints is over. Now courageous leadership is needed.

The Panel of Eminent Persons on United Nations–Civil Society Relations warned almost fifteen years ago that the United Nations must do more to strengthen global governance and tackle democratic deficits. The Panel stressed that more systematic engagement of parliamentarians, national parliaments and local authorities in the United Nations would strengthen global governance, confront democratic deficits in intergovernmental affairs, buttress representational democracy and connect the United Nations better with global opinion. Current arrangements are not adequate.

When the international Campaign for a United Nations Parliamentary Assembly was launched eleven years ago, the campaign's patron, the late former United Nations Secretary-General Boutros Boutros-Ghali said that we need to promote the democratization of globalization, before globalization destroys the foundations of national and international democracy.

It is with great concern that we are now witnessing how this exact development is unfolding. As the former Secretary-General stated, the establishment of a Parliamentary Assembly at the United Nations has become an indispensable step to achieve democratic control of globalization.

We, the undersigning members of parliament, affirm our commitment to the goal of creating a United Nations Parliamentary Assembly in order to strengthen the democratic representation of the world's citizens in global affairs and the UN's decision-making.

We invite our fellow parliamentarians from across the world who are democratically elected to join our Parliamentary Group for a UNPA in order to strengthen and coordinate our efforts. Together we can help build the political momentum and pressure that is needed to achieve our goal.

We believe that the upcoming 75th anniversary of the United Nations in 2020 must be used as an opportunity to take stock and initiate far-reaching reforms, including the establishment of a United Nations Parliamentary Assembly.

We call on the United Nations Secretary-General, the President of the United Nations General Assembly, the heads of states and governments and their foreign ministers as well as the representatives of United Nations member states in New York to initiate and support necessary steps in preparation of a meaningful UN Reform Summit in 2020 and towards the creation of a United Nations Parliamentary Assembly.

2. Parliamentary documents

Excerpts from European Parliament resolutions[222]

Adopted on 5 July 2018:[223]

[The European Parliament recommends to the Council] to advocate the establishment of a United Nations Parliamentary Assembly (UNPA) within the UN system in order to increase the democratic character, the democratic accountability and the transparency of global governance and to allow for better citizen participation in the activities of the UN and, in particular, to contribute to the successful implementation of the UN Agenda 2030 and the SDGs.

Adopted on 5 July 2017:[224]

[The European Parliament recommends to the Council] to foster a debate on the topic of the role of parliaments and regional assemblies in the UN system and on the topic of establishing a United Nations Parliamentary Assembly with a view to increasing the democratic profile and internal democratic process of the organization and to allow world civil society to be directly associated in the decision-making process.

---

[222] In descending chronological order.
[223] Resolution P8_TA (2018) 0312, para. m.
[224] Resolution P8_TA (2017) 0304, para. bm.

Adopted on 8 June 2011:[225]

[The European Parliament recommends to the Council] (be) to foster a debate on the topic of the role of parliaments and regional assemblies in the UN system, which is expected to feature on the agenda of the 66th UNGA session, and on the topic of establishing a United Nations Parliamentary Assembly (UNPA); further, to promote interaction on global issues between governments and parliaments,

(bf) to advocate the establishment of a UNPA within the UN system in order to increase the democratic nature, the democratic accountability and the transparency of global governance and to allow for greater public participation in the activities of the UN, acknowledging that a UNPA would be complementary to existing bodies, including the Inter-Parliamentary Union.

Adopted on 6 June 2005:[226]

[The European Parliament] calls for the establishment of a United Nations Parliamentary Assembly (UNPA) within the UN system, which would increase the democratic profile and internal democratic process of the organization and allow world civil society to be directly associated in the decisionmaking process; states that the Parliamentary Assembly should be vested with genuine rights of information, participation and control, and should be able to adopt recommendations directed at the UN General Assembly.

Adopted on 29 January 2004:[227]

[The European Parliament] invites the UN Secretary-General and the UN's political bodies, its Agencies, Funds and Programmes, to extend the current practices of dialogue, cooperation and coordination with the EU Council and Commission to the European Parliament, by: [...] jointly launching, in cooperation with regional or world Parliamentary Assemblies (e.g. the Inter-Parliamentary Union, the Council of Europe Parliamentary Assembly) a network of parliamentarians, which should meet on a regular basis in a Consultative Parliamentary Assembly under the United Nations, to discuss major political issues related to the UN's activity and the challenges it faces.

---

[225] Resolution P7_TA (2011) 0255.
[226] Resolution P6_TA (2005) 0237, para. 39.
[227] Resolution P5_TA (2004) 0037, para. 39, item 4.

Adopted on 23 March 1999:[228]

[The European Parliament] 10. Therefore proposes the introduction of a parliamentary dimension into the system of the UN organizations by creating parliamentary bodies composed of the chairmen of parliamentary committees of national and regional parliaments, starting e.g. with Environment and Foreign Affairs, thus strengthening the existing cooperation between the United Nations and the International Interparliamentary Union;

   11. Hopes that by creating such parliamentary accountability at world level the UN could become more relevant in the parliaments of the world.

Adopted on 8 February 1994:[229]

[The European Parliament] wishes consideration to be given to the possibility of setting up within the UN a parliamentary consultative assembly to enable the elected representatives of peoples to participate more fully in the work of UN bodies.

Pan-African Parliament

Resolution adopted on 12 May 2016[230]

[The Pan-African Parliament]
   Having regard to the PAP resolution on a UNPA adopted on 24 October 2007;
   Recalling its commitment to achieve the creation of a consultative UNPA within the United Nations (UN) system in accordance with Article 22 of the Charter of the United Nations that empowers the UN General Assembly to establish subsidiary bodies;
   Reaffirming its view that a UNPA is necessary to strengthen democratic participation and representation of the world's citizens in the UN;
   Convinced that a UNPA will contribute to strengthening democratic oversight over UN operations, particularly in Africa;
   Reiterating that a UNPA as parliamentary body of the UN system can significantly complement the valuable work of the Inter-Parliamentary Union, the umbrella organization of national parliaments;

---

[228] Resolution A4-0077/99.
[229] Resolution A3-0331/93, para. 17.
[230] Resolution PAP.4/PL/Recom.03(II). First three and last para. omitted here.

Noting that a UNPA is indispensable for the realization of the right of all to participation in global decision-making as stated in the UN General Assembly's resolutions on the promotion of a democratic and equitable international order, most recently A/RES/70/149 of 17 December 2015;

Welcoming the efforts of the International Campaign for a UNPA that was launched in 2007;

Noting that all regional supranational organizations have included parliamentary institutions in their institutional architecture as a means to ensure meaningful and effective peoples' participation and involvement in the affairs of the said regional organizations;

Further noting with concern that the creation of a UNPA is currently not part of the official UN reform agenda;

Therefore calls on the African Union and its Member States to support the creation of a UNPA and to take necessary steps to advance this goal at the UN by triggering and initializing a preparatory intergovernmental process for the purpose of establishing a UNPA;

Recommends that the African Union develops and advance a common African position on the matter;

Resolution adopted on 24 October 2007[231]

[The Pan-African Parliament]:

3. Further considering the growing role of international organizations such as the United Nations and its specialized organizations such as UNDP, UNICEF, UNHCR, WHO and FAO in key sectors such as peace and security, economic development, health, education and environment;

4. Stressing, in this context, that a growing number of decisions affecting the African Union's citizens are taken beyond the borders of their nation state;

5. Further noting that parliamentarians of the African Union's member states are often not included in national delegations to major international summits and negotiations, leading to knowledge gaps and missed opportunities for increased legitimacy and transparency of international decision-making;

6. Bearing in mind the opening words of the Charter of the United Nations "We the Peoples of the United Nations" which invoke the principle of democracy and root the legitimacy of the organization in the will of the peoples of its Member States;

---

[231] Adopted at the 8th Ordinary Session, Midrand, South Africa. First two para. omitted here.

7. Recalling the elaborations in the Report of the Panel of Eminent Persons on United Nations–Civil Society Relations mandated by the then United Nations Secretary- General published 11 June 2004 on the deficits of democracy in Global Governance, recommending a framework for global governance with democratic accountability to citizens;

8. Considering that if democratization is a major means to legitimize and improve national governance, it is also the most reliable way to legitimize and improve international organization, making it more open and responsive by increasing participation;

9. Noting that in contrast to regional international bodies such as the African Union, the European Union, the Council of Europe, or Mercosur, the United Nations and its specialized organizations is one of the last international fora lacking an integrated and institutionalized Parliamentary Assembly;

10. Taking note that the Common African Position on the Proposed Reform of the United Nations ("The Ezulwini Consensus") adopted at the 7th Extraordinary Session of the African Union's Executive Council in Addis Ababa, Ethiopia, from March 07 to 08, 2005, does not include positions on the shaping of a parliamentary dimension of the United Nations;

Therefore 11. Recommends that the Pan-African Parliament develop a common African position regarding the further development of citizen's involvement in international affairs and in particular in the United Nations and its specialized organizations, thereby addressing the growing democracy deficit in international foras;

12. Thereby recommends further that the Pan-African Parliament takes the initiative to achieve the establishment of a consultative United Nations Parliamentary Assembly (UNPA) within the UN system according to Article 22 of the Charter of the United Nations which enables the UN General Assembly to establish subsidiary bodies;

13. Notes that in a first preliminary step the United Nations Parliamentary Assembly could be composed of national parliamentarians, but that eventually it should be directly elected by universal adult suffrage in the UN member states, following the example of the provisions in Article 2 (3) of the Protocol to the Treaty Establishing the African Economic Community Relating to the Pan-African Parliament;

14. Stresses that a United Nations Parliamentary Assembly eventually should have participation and oversight rights, in particular, to send fully participating parliamentary delegations or representatives to international governmental fora and negotiations and to establish inquiry committees to assess

matters related to the actions of the United Nations, its personell and its special programmes;

15. Stresses further the potential of a United Nations Parliamentary Assembly to increase the efficiency, transparency and democratic character of the United Nations and international co-operation, thereby also increasing the participatory rights of the African Union's citizens;

16. Resolves that the establishment of a United Nations Parliamentary Assembly as envisaged before in no way contradics the valueable and highly esteemed work of the Inter-Parliamentary Union whose aim it is, in particular, to foster contacts, coordination and the exchange of experience among Parliaments and parliamentarians of all countries and to consider questions of international interest and express its views on such issues with the aim of bringing about action by national parliaments and their members.

East African Legislative Assembly resolution of 29 January 2013[232]

Appreciating the importance and good example of regional and sub-regional parliamentary assemblies in promoting the interests of citizens in regional and sub-regional intergovernmental organizations and thus in strengthening the democratic character of these organizations;

Recognizing the growing role and involvement of international organizations such as the United Nations and its specialized agencies in key sectors such as the promotion of peace and security, economic development, health, education, the environment or sustainable development;

Noting that no formal parliamentary body exists at the United Nations that would allow for popularly elected parliamentarians to take part in its deliberations;

Considering that the insufficient formal involvement of elected representatives in the work of the United Nations due to the absence of a parliamentary Assembly limits the democratic legitimacy of the world organization;

Aware of the concerted international efforts aimed at the establishment of a United Nations Parliamentary Assembly;

Further aware that the Pan-African Parliament, on the 24th October 2007, adopted a resolution recommending the adoption of a common African position on the establishment of a United Nations Parliamentary Assembly;

Further aware that this initiative is supported by other Parliamentary and Inter-Parliamentary bodies worldwide;

---

[232] First four para. omitted here.

Convinced that a United Nations Parliamentary Assembly would improve the transparency, accountability and the effectiveness of the United Nations;

Noting that a United Nations Parliamentary Assembly could be established simply by a vote of the United Nations General Assembly in accordance with Article 22 of the Charter of the United Nations without an amendment of the United Nations Charter;

This Assembly does resolve as follows: That it:

1. Supports the establishment of a United Nations Parliamentary Assembly based on equity and mutual trust.

2. Welcomes the Resolution of the Pan African Parliament and such other Parliaments and bodies that have pronounced themselves on this matter.

3. Urges the Partner States of the East African Community to take the initiative to promote the development of a common African position in support of the establishment of a United Nations Parliamentary Assembly.

Parliament of Mercosur resolution of 2 December 2011

Observing

1. In order to ensure international cooperation, the acceptance and legitimacy of the international order, and to improve its capacity to act, the citizens of the world must be effectively integrated into the United Nations (UN) system. To this end, they need to participate in its activities and decisions, incorporating the principle of democratic representation into the aspirations of the international community.

2. A UN Parliamentary Assembly would not be just another institution. As a voice of the citizens, it would be the expression and vehicle of a transformation of global consciousness and a facilitator for the understanding of the problems of international politics. Complex challenges posed by the globalization of economic and social processes, such as global social inequalities, the proliferation of weapons of mass destruction, global terrorism, global warming and financial volatility, can only be met by the gradual application of the democratic principle at international level.

3. In addition to the maintenance of international peace and security, the United Nations is required under article 10 of its Charter to promote international cooperation in economic, social, cultural or humanitarian matters and respect for human rights and fundamental freedoms. To this end, and without the need to amend any of the 111 articles of the UN Charter, its General Assembly can create a consultative parliamentary assembly, thus promoting the establishment of an important link between the United Nations, its agencies, governments, national parliamentarians and civil society:

4. A United Nations Parliamentary Assembly (UNPA) would facilitate the formation of a growing global network of parliamentarians and non-governmental organizations that would promote the representativeness of the United Nations and enhance its responsive capacities on the international stage. The establishment of such an institution would be a decisive step in the consolidation of the UN system, in the democratization of globalization, the globalization of democracy and the construction of a more just, peaceful and humane world.

Considering

That the space of national democracies is being restricted and threatened by the emergence of powerful global actors. On the other hand, we are also witnessing the emergence of international political organizations, in which only powerful and rich countries have representation, which places outside the global governance system the majority of the planet's inhabitants, who live in semi-developed or underdeveloped nations. It is the responsibility of all political bodies and especially of national and regional parliaments to assume their duties in defending the principles of democratic politics, which implies the application of their representative and parliamentary principles in each and every one where decisions affecting the life and well-being of the world's citizens must be taken.

For all these reasons, the Mercosur parliament expresses its support for the establishment of a United Nations Parliamentary Assembly and for the efforts towards its creation.

Declaring

1. Its support for the creation of a Parliamentary Assembly within the United Nations (UN) in order to strengthen the effectiveness, transparency, representativeness, plurality and legitimacy of the institutions that make up the UN system.

2. Its support of the efforts towards its formation.

Parliamentary Assembly of the Council of Europe

Adopted on 1 October 2009 (excerpt)[233]

4. The Assembly notes the numerous reform proposals that have been advanced during recent years and pays tribute to former United Nations Secretary-General Kofi Annan for his efforts to promote a comprehensive reform of the organization.

---

[233] Resolution 1688 (2009).

5. However, the Assembly regrets that there has so far been no reform proposal aimed at improving the democratic character of the United Nations. In this context, the Assembly recalls its well-established position in support of the introduction of a parliamentary dimension of the United Nations, as set forth in its Resolution 1476 (2006) on the parliamentary dimension of the United Nations, in order to improve the transparency, accountability and democratic oversight of the organization and bridge the gap between the United Nations and the public.

6. The incorporation of a democratic element into the United Nations system has become even more necessary as a response to the process of globalisation: only global governance can face up to its challenges, and such global governance, embodied in the United Nations, must be based on democratic principles.

7. As to institutional reform, the Assembly reiterates its conviction that the role and the authority of the United Nations General Assembly as "the premier decision-making and political body of the United Nations" should be restored. This role could be further strengthened by the introduction, or the reinforcement, of a parliamentary element in the structure of the UN General Assembly, composed of either representatives of the parliamentary assemblies of each country or directly elected representatives.

Adopted on 23 January 2006 (excerpt)[234]

3. At this crucial moment, the Assembly calls for a renewed impetus in the continuation of the UN reform process. In its view, a durable and forward-looking reform should be led by the objective of rendering the whole United Nations system more transparent, legitimate and accountable before its member states as well as public opinion at large. For this reason, the reform cannot be limited to making the organization more reflective of current geopolitical realities but should aim at incorporating democratic mechanisms in the UN system, with a view to redressing the democratic deficit in global governance and bring the United Nations closer to the people.

4. In this context, the Assembly believes that the issue of the closer involvement of parliamentarians in UN activities should be brought to the forefront of the current reform discussions as it is a fundamental means to associate the people – through their elected representatives – to the UN deliberative process, the oversight of UN activities and the monitoring of the implementation of UN decisions by member states.

---

[234] Resolution 1476 (2006).

5. Parliamentary involvement in the work of the UN should be enhanced progressively. This process should begin through the setting up within national parliaments of groups of members of parliament to support cooperation with the United Nations, by ensuring that parliamentarians are fully informed of UN activities. The process should culminate with the inclusion in the UN system of a parliamentary assembly with consultative functions.

6. The Assembly takes note of the recommendations put forward in the report of the Panel of Eminent Persons on United Nations-Civil Society Relations – the so-called Cardoso report – concerning the engagement of parliamentarians in UN work and welcomes the growing association of parliamentarians with UN activities, in the form of strengthened cooperation between the United Nations and the Inter-Parliamentary Union (IPU).

7. This strengthened cooperation is welcome as it improves the familiarity of national parliamentarians with UN activities and provides them with a podium in UN instances. The Assembly, however, believes that in order to have a lasting impact on the legitimacy, accountability and representativity of the United Nations system, the involvement of parliamentarians in UN work should be further developed so as to become systematic and structurally linked with the functioning of UN institutions. In particular, given its deliberative and oversight functions as well as its role as the most representative global forum, the UN General Assembly is ideally placed to act as an interface with parliamentarians.

8. A decisive step towards the development of a UN parliamentary dimension could be the establishment of an experimental parliamentary committee with consultative functions for General Assembly committees. It would be composed of national delegations, elected by national parliaments, with due respect to the principle of representativity of the different political forces present in parliament and with due consideration to gender balance. This parliamentary committee should be of reasonable size and ensure a fair geographical representation of all the regional groupings currently existing in the General Assembly. Within each regional grouping, national delegations would rotate on a periodic basis. Should this experiment be successful, the structure and functioning of this committee could inspire the establishment of a UN parliamentary assembly with consultative functions for the plenary General Assembly.

9. In light of the above, the Assembly urges Council of Europe member and observer states to:

9.1. encourage debates on issues discussed at the UN in national parliaments as well as in regional parliamentary assemblies;

9.2. allow the active participation of parliamentarians in national delegations to the General Assembly.

10. In addition, the Assembly invites the UN Secretary-General to give further consideration to the recommendations of the Cardoso report concerning the engagement of parliamentarians and suggest proposals along the same lines.

11. Finally, the Assembly invites the UN General Assembly to:

11.1. envisage appropriate ways for involving parliamentarians in its activities by:

11.1.1. working with the IPU and other interparliamentary representative bodies and devising a step-by-step strategy, which could include the following stages:

11.1.1.1. setting up a network of regional parliamentary assemblies to discuss emerging UN priorities, with consultative functions for one or more General Assembly committees;

11.1.1.2. setting up a parliamentary committee to discuss issues of special global or regional importance and/or the UN budget, with consultative functions for one or more General Assembly committees;

11.1.1.3. setting up a UN parliamentary assembly, based on national delegations, with consultative functions for the General Assembly;

11.1.1.4. setting up, together with the United Nations and its institutions, of national information and research centres for parliamentarians, local government representatives, representatives of NGOs and volunteers in member states;

11.1.2. adopting clear rules for the involvement of parliamentarians in its work, setting out their rights and responsibilities, as well as the obligation for parliamentary delegations to ensure a fair representation of the political parties or groups in their parliament and give due account to gender balance considerations;

11.1.3. setting up a panel to make precise proposals on the recommended size, composition and rota system of parliamentary committees and/or a UN parliamentary assembly;

11.2. consider additional measures to ensure better interaction between the General Assembly and national or regional parliaments, in particular those encouraging the more active involvement of the Speakers or Presidents of these assemblies in the work of the regional groupings of the General Assembly.

Latin-American Parliament resolution of 5 December 2008[235]

Considering

The principle of defending democracy which governs the activities of the Latin-American Parliament, in accordance with article 3 of the Statute.

The purpose of defending the full implementation of freedom, social justice, economic independence and the exercise of representative and participatory democracy, with strict adherence to the principles of non intervention and free self-determination of the countries, expressed in article 4 of the Parlatino Statute.

The declaration of the Committee of Political and Municipal Affairs and of Integration of the Latin American Parliament, approved last 12th June in the city of Bogota, expressing its support for establishing a Parliamentary Assemby of the United Nations.

Whereas

That to guarantee international cooperation, acceptance and legitimacy of the United Nations, and to reinforce its capacity to act, human beings should be directly and effectively integrated in the UN and its agencies, which requires that they are allowed to participate in its activities.

That without the need of amending the Charter of the United Nations, an Assembly of this kind can create an important link between the United Nations, its agencies, national governments and parliaments and civil society.

The XXIV. Ordinary Assembly of the Latin-American Parliament declares

1. Its support to efforts towards the creation and establishment of a Parliamentary Assembly of the United Nations Organization (UNO) with the purpose of strengthening the effectiveness, transparency, representativeness, plurality and legitimacy of the international system.

2. Its absolute belief in the legitimacy of the decisions taken as a result of participatory, pluralist and democratic deliberation, an unavoidable condition of the effective implementation of policies which benefit our countries.

---

[235] XXIV. Ordinary Assembly meeting in Panamá, declaration no. 10.

Literature and sources

AFP. (2019, May 24). Council of Europe assembly rejects far-right political grouping.

African Union. (2014). Protocol to the Constitutive Act of the African Union relating to the Pan-African Parliament. Adopted by the 23rd Ordinary Session of the Assembly of Heads of State and Government, Malabo, Equatorial Guinea.

Altman, S. A., Ghemawat, P., & Bastian, P. (2019). DHL Global Connectedness Index 2018: The State of Globalization in a Fragile World. DHL. (www.dpdhl.com)

Beyme, K. von. (1998). Niedergang der Parlamente. Internationale Politik, 4, 21–30.

Bieber, R., Jacqué, J.-P., & Weiler, J. H. H. (Eds.). (1985). An ever closer Union. A critical analysis of the Draft Treaty establishing the European Union. Commission of the European Communities. (cadmus.eui.eu)

Boutros-Ghali, B. (1996). Supplement to reports on democratization. Report to the 51st Session of the United Nations General Assembly. UN Doc. A/51/761.

Boutros-Ghali, B. (2007). Message to the Campaign for a UN Parliamentary Assembly. (www.unpacampaign.org, reprinted on p. 129)

Bummel, A. (2010a). The composition of a Parliamentary Assembly at the United Nations (3rd edition). Committee for a Democratic UN (now DWB).

Bummel, A. (2010b). Developing International Democracy - For a Parliamentary Assembly at the United Nations (2nd ed.). Komitee für eine demokratische UNO (now DWB).

Bummel, A. (2014). A World Parliament and the Transition from International Law to World Law. Cadmus, 2(3), 121–128.

Bummel, A. (2018). A Renewed World Organization for the 21st Century. Democracy Without Borders, Discussion Paper. (www.democracywithoutborders.org/files/-DWBGCFAB.pdf)

Bummel, A. (2019). The Case for a UN Parliamentary Assembly and the Inter-Parliamentary Union. Democracy Without Borders, Policy Review. (www.democracywithoutborders.org/files/DWBIPUAB.pdf)

Bummel, A., Kerr, D., & Iglesias, F. (2010). Democratizing Global Climate Policy through a UN Parliamentary Assembly. Paper presented at the conference "Democratizing Climate Governance" at the Australian National University, 15-16 July 2010.

Bundesverfassungsgericht. (1993, Oct 12). BVerfGE 89, 155, 2 BvR 2134, 2159/92 (Maastricht).

Bundesverfassungsgericht. (2009, June 30). BVerfG, 2 BvE 2/08 (Treaty of Lisbon).

Cabrera, L. (2018). The Case for a United Nations Parliamentary Assembly as a Means of Promoting Just Security. In W. Durch, J. Larik, & R. Ponzio (Eds.), Just Security in an Undergoverned World (pp. 413–439). Oxford University Press.

Childers, E., & Urquhart, B. (1994). Renewing the United Nations System. Dag Hammarskjöld Foundation. (www.dhf.uu.se)

Chowla, P., Oatham, J., & Wren, C. (2007). Bridging the democratic deficit: Double majority decision making and the IMF. One World Trust and Bretton Woods Project.

Clark, G., & Sohn, L. B. (1966). World Peace Through World Law. Two Alternative Plans (Third Edition Enlarged). Harvard University Press.

Cofelice, A. (2019). Parliamentary Institutions in Regional and International Governance. Routledge.

Commission on Global Governance. (1995). Our Global Neighborhood. Oxford University Press.

Commission on Global Security, Justice & Governance. (2015). Confronting the Crisis of Global Governance. The Hague Institute for Global Justice and The Stimson Center.

Corbett, R. (2001). The European Parliament's role in closer EU integration (First paperback edition). Palgrave.

Costa, O. (2016). The history of European electoral reform and the Electoral Act 1976. European Parliament History Series. European Parliamentary Research Service.

Council of Europe. (2018, Apr 15). Report of the Independent Investigation Body on the allegations of corruption within the Parliamentary Assembly.

CUNPA (2007a). Appeal for the establishment of a Parliamentary Assembly at the United Nations. (www.unpacampaign.org, reprinted on p. 128)

CUNPA. (2007b). Conclusions regarding policies of the Campaign for a UN Parliamentary Assembly. (www.unpacampaign.org, reprinted on p. 130)

CUNPA. (2008). The establishment of a United Nations Parliamentary Assembly and the Inter-Parliamentary Union. (www.unpacampaign.org, reprinted on p. 131)

CUNPA. (2009). Call for global democratic oversight of international financial and economic institutions. (www.unpacampaign.org, reprinted on p. 132)

CUNPA. (2010). Declaration of Buenos Aires. (www.unpacampaign.org, reprinted on p. 133)

CUNPA. (2013). Declaration of Brussels: Toward a democratic and equitable international order. (www.unpacampaign.org, reprinted on p. 134)

CUNPA (2018). Call to Action on the Creation of a UN Parliamentary Assembly (www.unpacampaign.org, reprinted on p. 137)

Deplano, R. (2019). The Parliament of the World? Reflections on the Proposal to Establish a United Nations Parliamentary Assembly. Leiden Journal of International Law, forthcoming 2020. (papers.ssrn.com/abstract=3490887)

Deutscher Bundestag. (2005). Für eine parlamentarische Mitwirkung im System der Vereinten Nationen. Drucksache 15/5690.

DWB. (2019, Nov 1). The vision of a World Parliament promoted during global action week. Blog. (www.democracywithoutborders.org/11973/)

Economist Intelligence Unit. (2006). The Economist Intelligence Unit's Index of Democracy 2006.

Economist Intelligence Unit. (2020). Democracy Index 2019: A year of democratic setbacks and popular protest.

Einstein, A. (1960). Open Letter to the General Assembly of the United Nations, October 1947. In O. Nathan & H. Norden (Eds.), Einstein on Peace (pp. 440–443). Simon and Schuster.

EP. (1984). Draft Treaty establishing the European Union adopted on 14 February 1984. Bulletin of the European Communities, 27(C77), 33–54. (eur-lex.europa.eu)

EP. (2005). Resolution on the reform of the United Nations. P6_TA (2005) 0237 (see excerpt on p. 139).

EP. (2008). Towards a reform of the World Trade Organization. P6_TA (2008) 0180.

EP. (2011). 66th Session of the United Nations General Assembly. P7_TA (2011) 0255. (see excerpt on p. 139)

EP. (2018). Recommendation to the Council on the 73rd Session of the United Nations General Assembly. P8_TA (2018) 0312. (see excerpt on p. 138)

EP. (2019a, Jan 31). European Parliament approves more transparency and efficiency in its internal rules. Press release. (www.europarl.europa.eu)

EP. (2019b). Understanding the d'Hondt method. Briefing of the European Parliamentary Research Service. (www.europarl.europa.eu)

European Court of Justice (2001, Oct 2). Joined Cases T-222/99, T-327/99 and T-329/99. Martinez and others vs Parliament. Judgement of the Court of First Instance. (eur-lex.europa.eu)

Falk, R., & Strauss, A. (2011). A Global Parliament: Essays and Articles. Committee for a Democratic UN (now DWB).

Freedom House. (2000). Freedom in the World 2000. (freedomhouse.org/report/freedom-world/freedom-world-2000)

Freedom House. (2019). Freedom in the World 2019. (freedomhouse.org)

Global Challenges Foundation. (2017). Attitudes to global risks and governance.

Global Challenges Foundation. (2018). Attitudes to global risk and governance survey 2018.

Global Greens. (2008, May 4). 21 Commitments for the 21st Century. Declaration adopted at the Global Greens Second Congress in Sao Paulo, Brazil.

Global Greens. (2012). For Global Democracy and a United Nations Parliamentary Assembly. Resolution adopted at the Global Greens Third Congress, Dakar, Senegal, March 29-April 1, 2012.

GlobeScan Incorporated. (2005). Global Issues Monitor 2005.

Guterres, A. (2018, Sep. 25). Address to the General Assembly, New York. (gadebate.un.org/sites/default/files/gastatements/73/unsg_en.pdf).

Habermas, J. (1995). Kants Idee des Ewigen Friedens aus dem historischen Abstand von 200 Jahren. Kritische Justiz, 28(3), 293–319.

Havel, V. (2000, Sep. 8). Address of the President of the Czech Republic at the Millennium Summit of the United Nations.

Heinrich, D. (2010). The Case for a UN Parliamentary Assembly. Committee for a Democratic UN (now DWB). Extended reprint, originally published 1992.

Höffe, O. (2002). Demokratie im Zeitalter der Globalisierung (1. überarbeitete und aktualisierte Neuausgabe). C.H. Beck.

ILO. (2004). A fair globalization: Creating opportunities for all. Report of the World Commission on the Social Dimension of Globalization.

IPU. (2018, Sep 12). 2019 Consolidated Budget. 139th IPU Assembly and Related Meetings. EX/280/10(b)-P.1. (ipu.org)

Kaiser, W. (2018). Shaping European Union: The European Parliament and Institutional Reform, 1979-1989. European Parliament History Series. European Parliamentary Research Service.

Kissling, C. (2006). Die Interparlamentarische Union im Wandel. Rechtspolitische Ansätze einer repräsentativ-parlamentarischen Gestaltung der Weltpolitik. Peter Lang.

Kissling, C. (2011). The Legal and Political Status of International Parliamentary Institutions. Committee for a Democratic UN.

Kull, S. (2010). Listening to the Voice of Humanity. Kosmos Journal, Spring-Summer, 26–29.

Leinen, J. (2019). Fake Groups in the European Parliament. What Makes a Group a Group and Why Are Fake Groups a Problem? Federalist Debate, XXXII(2), 10–14.

Leinen, J., & Bummel, A. (2018). A World Parliament: Governance and Democracy in the 21st Century. Democracy Without Borders.

Leinen, J., & Bummel, A. (2019). Weltinnenpolitik und Weltparlament: Anforderungen an eine Weltrechtsordnung. S+F Sicherheit und Frieden, 4, 198–202.

Liberal International. (2005, May 14). Strengthening citizens representation on international level through an UN Parliamentary Assembly. (Resolution adopted by the 53rd Congress in Sofia, Bulgaria).

Lopez-Claros, A., Dahl, A. L., & Groff, M. (2020). Global Governance and the Emergence of Global Institutions for the 21st Century. Cambridge University Press.

Monbiot, G. (2004). The Age of Consent. Manifesto for a New World Order. Harper Perennial.

New Vision. (2019, Oct 15). African Union slashes PAP budget by $4m. (www.newvision.co.ug)

Norris, P. (2011). Democratic deficit: Critical citizens revisited. Cambridge University Press.

Organ, J., & Murphy, B. (2019). A Voice for Global Citizens: A UN World Citizens' Initiative. Democracy Without Borders, Democracy International, CIVICUS: World Alliance for Citizen Participation.

PACE. (2000, Sep 27). The United Nations at the turn of the new century. Recommendation 1476 (2000).

PACE. (2006). Parliamentary dimension of the United Nations. Resolution 1476 (2006). (reprinted on p. 146)

PACE. (2017). Expenditure of the Parliamentary Assembly for the biennium 2018-2019. Resolution 2165 (2017).

PAP. (2007). A United Nations Parliamentary Assembly. Resolution adopted at the 8th Ordinary Session, Midrand, South Africa. (reprinted on p. 141)

Parlamento del Mercosur. (2011, Dec 2). Apoyo al establecimiento de una Asamblea Parlamentaria de las Naciones Unidas. MERCOSUR/PM/SP/DECL. 01/2011 (reprinted on p. 144).

Penrose, L. S. (1946). The Elementary Statistics of Majority Voting. Journal of the Royal Statistical Society, 109(1), 53–57.

Piodi, F. (2007). Towards a single parliament. The influence of the ECSC Common Assembly on the Treaties of Rome. Archive and Documentation Centre (CARDOC). European Parliament Directorate-General for the Presidency.

Piodi, F. (2009). Towards direct elections to the European Parliament. Archive and Documentation Centre (CARDOC). European Parliament Directorate-General for the Presidency.

Pirate Parties International. (2013, Apr 21). Kazan declaration of the Pirate Parties International.

Rocabert, J., Schimmelfennig, F., Crasnic, L., & Winzen, T. (2019). The rise of international parliamentary institutions: Purpose and legitimation. The Review of International Organizations, 14(4), 607–631.

Rockström, J., & et.al. (2009). Planetary Boundaries: Exploring the Safe Operating Space for Humanity. Ecology and Society, 14(2), 32.

Šabič, Z. (2008). Building Democratic and Responsible Global Governance: The Role of International Parliamentary Institutions. Parliamentary Affairs, 61(2), 255–271.

Savio, R. (2019, Oct. 7). Farewell to the World Social Forum? Great Transition Initiative. (greattransition.org/gti-forum/wsf-savio).

Schermers, H. G., & Blokker, N. (2018). International Institutional Law. Brill Nijhoff.

Schneckener, U., & Rinke, B. (2012). Informalisierung der Weltpolitik? Regieren durch Clubs. In Stiftung Entwicklung und Frieden (Ed.), Globale Trends 2013 (pp. 27–42). Fischer.

Schwartzberg, J. (2012). Creating a World Parliamentary Assembly. An Evolutionary Journey. Committee for a Democratic UN (now DWB).

Schwartzberg, J. (2013). Transforming the United Nations System. Designs for a Workable World. United Nations University Press.

Sharei, S.-Y. (2018, May 4). United Nations charter reform and the unfulfilled promise of San Francisco. Democracy Without Borders, Blog. (www.democracywithoutborders.org/5510/)

Socialist International (2005). Reforming the United Nations. For a New Global Agenda. (Position paper adopted at the SI Council, Tel Aviv and Ramallah, 23-24 May, 2005).

Socialist International. (2003, Oct 29). Governance in a Global Society – The Social Democratic Approach (Report adopted at the XXII. Congress, São Paulo).

Sohn, L. B. (Ed.). (1970). The United Nations: The Next Twenty-Five Years. Twentieth Report of the Commission to Study the Organization of Peace. Oceana Publications.

Soros, G. (1998). The Crisis of Global Capitalism. PublicAffairs.

Spiegel, P. (2009). Mit einem UN-Parlament demokratische Prinzipien bei globalen Entscheidungen durchsetzen. In F. J. Radermacher, M. Obermüller, & P. Spiegel (Eds.), Global Impact: Der neue Weg zur globalen Verantwortung (pp. 235–257). Hanser.

Stamelos, C. (2020). Jurisprudence (Philosophy of Law), Nomiki Bibliothiki [in Greek].

Stimson Center. (2020). UN 2.0: Ten Innovations for Global Governance—75 Years beyond San Francisco.

Streit, C. K. (1939). Union Now. A Proposal for a Federal Union of the Democracies of the North Atlantic. Jonathan Cape.

Synovate. (2007, Aug). BBC Poll: Why Democracy.

Tenbergen, R. (2018). United Humans. Democracy Without Borders, Discussion Paper. (www.democracywithoutborders.org/5776/)

UN. (1950). Uniting for peace. A/RES/377(V).

UN. (2000). United Nations Millennium Declaration. A/RES/55/2.

UN. (2004). We the Peoples: Civil society, the United Nations and Global Governance. Report of the Panel of Eminent Persons on United Nations–Civil Society Relations. A/58/817.

UN. (2006). Human Rights Council. A/RES/60/251.

UN. (2018a). Promotion of a democratic and equitable international order. A/RES/73/169.

UN. (2018b). Interaction between the United Nations, national parliaments and the Inter-Parliamentary Union. Report of the Secretary-General. A/72/791.

V-Dem Institute. (2019). Democracy facing global challenges. V-Dem Annual Democracy Report 2019.

Wike, R., Simmons, K., Stokes, B., & Fetterolf, J. (2017). Globally, Broad Support for Representative and Direct Democracy. Pew Research Center. (www.pewglobal.org)

Winter, T. v. (2005). Die Idee einer Parlamentarisierung der Vereinten Nationen als Beitrag zur Debatte über "Global Governance" und Demokratie. Info-Brief des Wissenschaftlichen Dienstes. Deutscher Bundestag.

9 783942 282178